A Tough Grace

Mental Illness As A Spiritual Path

To Leslie,
In celebration +
appreciation for
the shared journey,
Alice

ALICE A. HOLSTEIN, Ed.D

chipmunkapublishing
the mental health publisher

Alice A. Holstein

Published by
Chipmunkapublishing
PO Box 6872
Brentwood
Essex CM13 1ZT
United Kingdom

http://www.chipmunkapublishing.com

Edited by Aleks Lech

ISBN   978-1-84991-640-0

Chipmunkapublishing gratefully acknowledge the support of Arts Council England.

Dedication

This book is my brick in a "Vietnam Wall" we need somewhere to honor all who have suffered and still suffer from mental illness. The war we fight is noble, unheralded, unclaimed, full of sacrifice and pain. We need a place to trace the names of those who have been lost as well as those who suffer while we strive for a better way to see and treat mental illness.

This dedication is also for all those who personally helped me along the way, those who are known to me by name and especially all the ones unnamed. Without you, which surely number in the hundreds, I would not have made it through the wilderness.

Alice A. Holstein

Table of Contents

Alice A. Holstein

A Tough Grace

If a person is called to be spokesperson
for the inner world, he(she) is a healer
or prophet and must obey his(her) calling.

John Sanford
The Man Who Wrestled with God, p.52

Introduction

Living on the streets, periodically, when I was in
my late 50s and early 60s was horrifying. Not that I
didn't have assets. I did, but I either got separated from
them or was too paranoid to tap them, and often I was
so mentally "out of it" that I thought everything was lost.
The paranoia, a symptom of manic depression, made
me believe that there was a drug and vice conspiracy
operating everywhere. Thus, no place was safe and I
was driven by fear to travel far from home.
Consequently, I felt at times as though I was entirely
homeless. Not only was I a senior citizen and a
professional career woman ill-equipped to endure
hardship, but the medication side-effects had ballooned
me, temporarily, to 220 pounds.

Looking backward, I don't see now how I hauled
myself around or was able to escape serious harm or
survive on the streets for several months at a time. It is
a miracle that I survived at all, much less am thriving
now.

For nearly 30 years I've been consciously working
on myself to heal parental-societal wounds and survive
mental illness. No one told me that it would take so
much effort to do the inner work essential to living life
fully. No one told me that this kind of work would begin
in earnest at mid-life, absorbing me afterwards for

another 12 years with both intense suffering and breakthroughs as the manic depression unfolded. Yet no one told me either that doing the work, diligently, deeply, doggedly, would bring wisdom, creativity and fulfillment.

The fact that this kind of intense inner exploration remains outside the cultural norm makes me want to share my stories, both the good and the bad alike. Beneath my sometimes horrific challenges and manic messes lies a hero's journey of *separation, initiation and return* that Joseph Campbell described as myth throughout the centuries. The experience of this universal spiritual path is by no means unique but it is also somewhat unusual. Having to survive the rigors and burdens associated with manic depression cause me to unabashedly claim, not just survival, but a victory over an illness that affects millions and claims 15-20% of us as suicide victims. This does not mean that I'm "cured" or that I've given up medications, but it does mean emerging with a rare sense of rebirth. I've brought back from my descent into hell a new view of mental illness. There *is* an underlying wholeness to the recovery process that means we who suffer should not be treated as damaged goods, but rather as wounded souls struggling for healing and wholeness. Mental illness can be a kind of "tough grace,' a profound spiritual path. This is a revolutionary concept.

A new view is desperately needed, for the toll from mental illness is very high, whether money or torn families or blighted souls. Beyond the suicide statistics, many thousands die premature deaths from homelessness or from the side effects of the toxic, chemical stew they are forced to ingest to prevent manic episodes. Many suffer serious side-effects from medications that make them miserable, non-productive people; some do find "the right" medications to live productive lives, but thousands live at a fraction of their potential. The pain and damage that some people create in their wake can be substantial.

I believe these gruesome results can be significantly changed over the next 25 years. In the U.S. alone, manic depression is estimated to cost 45 billion and depression 44 billion. Most importantly, beyond the money, I believe that thousands of lives can be saved, whether from the high suicide rate or from things such as the four deaths caused by a student suffering from manic depression while careening down a street in California. Much domestic and other violence, drug usage, homelessness and alcoholism comes from undiagnosed or untreated manic depression. Thousands can be rescued from poverty and the disrupted family and economic lives that accompany this illness.

To do so, however, we need new eyes with which to see mental illness and the possibilities for evolved treatment methods. Much of the personal meaning behind my years of suffering is that I became a revolutionary during the course of doing battle with this monster called manic depression. I faced death many times, whether physical or psychological, had my life saved literally hundreds of time by acts large and small and fought my way beyond the traditional medical model to bring back a new paradigm for seeing the illness.

Having emerged from the wilderness, manic depression ultimately became my friend because it forced me to acquire the knowledge and skills that now produce creativity and inner happiness. The self-realization produced an inner strength, capable of saying "no" to the status quo in many ways at the same time that it softened me and enlarged my compassion. This profound spiritual path amounts to a very tough grace.

In this book I hope my stories will enlighten and give people hope. For a long time I didn't have that myself, or I lost it and had to create it over and over, but hope makes the difference in getting well or not.

Alice A .Holstein, Ed.D.
La Crosse, WI, 2011

A Tough Grace

While trauma can be hell on earth,
trauma resolved is a gift from the
gods---a heroic journey that
belongs to each of us.

Peter Levine
Waking the Tiger p.12

Chapter 1: Twelve Blurred Years

Memories blur. What year did this or that happen? Even if the year is clear, what were the other events that accompanied this or that incident? Memory lapses are common with this illness. Either I was "out of it" in delusions and paranoia or else the memories were buried under Post Traumatic Stress Disorder (PTSD). Some of them are conscious, but just too painful to share. I cannot be entirely naked even though I am fully out of the closet.

There was a time when I could hardly remember anything because I was so concerned with survival, so shell-shocked with my own bizarre behavior that I couldn't allow memories to surface. During several recoveries after a manic episode, there were nighttime flashbacks that prevented sleep, mortifying me with their evidence of genuine madness. Daylight was difficult too.

As I grew healthier, however, healing from more than a decade of suffering and chronic stress, more of the memories returned. This book will reconstruct portions of experience, combining the surreal and the real that weave the passage from madness to rebirth.

Manic depression is characterized by extreme, elated highs and depressive lows that follow. There are variations on this cyclical behavior that differ from person to person. My pattern was to have a manic episode periodically, often every nine months, or with barely a year in between, or even successively when I was wrongly medicated or allowed to leave the hospital before I was really well. Other people cycle in shorter time periods.

During the twelve years of almost unendurable suffering, from 1995-2006, I suffered several depressions that were so debilitating that I could barely function except to watch TV, sleep long hours and make the supreme effort to attend a weekly support group meeting. At least there was some salvation of hearing others with similar plights. At one meeting I heard about one man who bought seven Cadillac cars during an episode. This helped me live with the fact that I had bought a car I didn't need. (Throughout the course of the illness I would buy two others; that meant having to sell the car I already owned, often at a great loss.) Speaking my truth at those meetings was helpful rather than swallowing the pain. People understand in those environments and speak authentically from the heart. Knowing that one is not alone can be life-saving, plus finding the honesty that is missing in daily life can be restorative.

During depressions, the ability to make decisions ground to a halt. A number of ill-conceived ones were clearly irrational, such as modifying my bedroom closet as a "safe closet" should I need to hide again, or taking a small weapons defense course where I learned that my Air Force marksmanship rating had deteriorated to not being able to handle a pistol at all. Why take this course when I owned no gun and had no intention of buying one when I was my "normal" self? The lingering paranoia of the manic episode explains the nonsense.

Depression also meant being able to do only one or two things a day. Berating myself over this was common, but the lesson from the habit was to eventually learn not to push the river. I simply had to take life very slowly, taking as good care of myself as possible and allowing that to be acceptable.

The best of manic depression is its supra-normal aspects. The worst of mania is psychotic, a kind of living hell that is as hard to describe as are the highs. People commonly accuse us of liking those highs so much that we purposely go without medications, but my aftermaths were so damaging that I never felt that way. I stopped taking my meds several times because I was suffering so much from side-effects, but mostly I got separated from them or thought them poisoned in my paranoia. Most of my manic episodes occurred while I was on medications.

During the "good" phases of an episode, I experienced extraordinary synchronicity, moment-by-moment direction or decisions in a flow that seemed directed by a power greater than me. Everything was meaningful, including a series of "hidden languages" of colors, signs, symbols and signals. There were creative visions, telepathy and heightened love. High energy that often spiraled into sleep deprivation accompanied the excitement about a world of unusual sights, sounds and smells. Experiencing heightened stimuli is characteristic. There is enhanced ability to absorb it until the episode goes mysteriously sour.

During both the good and the bad periods, I talked either silently or outwardly to God, however you understand that term, sometimes railing like a drunken sailor at him/her if seemingly required to do something difficult. Just as often, however, there was comfort because this presence was the only company for days, weeks or months. The isolation came from being on the road and because most people seemed potentially harmful when I was paranoid. The comfort came from a palpable sense of being intimately close to a spiritual presence as well as sometimes to an upper spiritual realm or to departed spirits who were people once close to me. I talked to them too, sometimes resolving issues in an inner sense that marred our relationship while they lived.

All of this was not necessarily madness. Saints and mystics write of their closeness to God. Spiritual leader, Rudolph Steiner, wrote about a spiritual realm above us, and psychics regularly contact the dead who bring us messages, the nature of which are mysteriously clear to the psychic who "reads" them and us.

During the damaging parts of my episodes, which were sometimes concurrent with the positive aspects, I became argumentative, inappropriate in behavior or words, very paranoid, unable to be reached with logic although I also engaged in coherent conversations beneath the chaos of my mind. I was convinced that there was a gigantic drug and vice conspiracy operating everywhere and thus, every institution was unsafe and every possible helping source, such as police and hospitals, was contaminated with evil.

Extensive spending sprees were common. During them I accumulated many unneeded items, including strange gifts for a staff I believed should be assembled for special missions to help transform the world. Grandiosity is characteristic of mania. I also engaged in weird or dangerous behavior, such as reckless driving or steadily running from imagined danger and hiding in strange places. Sleep deprivation turned to the point of exhaustion; amnesia and forgetfulness were common. Invasive behavior with others occurred, such as unannounced visits, phone calls or wacky e-mails. I did damage to others' property. Often I trashed my home and files or packed it up as if to move out of the house. I wrote both coherent and incoherent messages to myself or imagined others. Some made no sense at all or were full of paranoia, mortifying me when I discovered them later. Some thoughts, however, now seem as right as they can be. My heightened state of mind saw so clearly that we have a huge capacity to heal numerous illnesses and to create our own reality with thoughts. Many with an immature world view do not realize the horror and havoc they create. This seems unvarnished truth now.

The bad times also brought the madness of seeing a world afflicted with drugs, child abuse, crime, pedophilia, group sex and obscene greed. There was, of course, truth in these insights, but the psychotic state meant that I saw the evidence everywhere, with no safety for me. They were all part of a giant vice ring and I was the hunted because I knew too much and had spoken about it openly. My hospital records testify to the fact that I talked about these things and feared them.

Over the course of 12 horrific years I spent some 6-8 months living on the streets in Colorado, Arizona, Minnesota and Wisconsin. Having once been a proud career woman with several prestigious clients in my consulting profession, I was reduced at times to being a genuine bag lady. I slept in several homeless and battered women's shelters, some cardboard boxes, on the cement and in many open fields. I spent time sleeping on the floor in a soup kitchen where we had thin pallets and one blanket, packed in like sardines when the weather outside dropped below freezing. Sometimes I walked all night to keep warm; I went hungry for five days one time and eight days another. I had three or four Chapter 51's (meaning when you are judged a danger to yourself or others, go to court and then are sentenced to various treatment stipulations). I had grandiose beliefs about my abilities or powers, plus delusions and impaired judgment.

After the episodes, the madness continued to wreak havoc. Knowing what you have done or said, both publicly and privately, is a living hell beyond imagination. How to reconcile these two selves, the one so out of alignment with the "normal" self we know? How can one bear the resulting shame and stigma? I call this the "psychic split" and sometimes it took me months to put the two selves back together again. It was an invisible pain that seemed nearly unbearable.

And then there is the wreckage to clean up, the physical messes to undo when one is exhausted or bearing medical bills that can break the back and spirit. I fouled my financial affairs, left things in places far from home that then had to be retrieved, and didn't let people know when I was hospitalized so that they worried terribly. How can we suffer the loneliness of disrupted jobs, friendship and community? How can we even get out of bed, tackle things one by one, want to go on at all when this is one more experience of crawling to our knees again?

In the early days it took forever to recover from a manic episode, punctuated by the depressions that made it far more difficult. In succeeding years the recovery came easier, faster, but so did the mania. As I went along, I cared less about the stigma and shame. This was due partly to the intense healing work I did and partly emerged over the course of time when I came out the other end of the hero's journey which I'll explain in Chapter 2. The self-stigma was lessening. I also learned to send "fence-mending" messages that explained the illness and expressed regret for the madness.

Beginning in 2002, I consciously reclaimed my life in earnest, re-framing experiences, pursuing healing on all fronts, looking for the lessons underneath, rejoicing in the evident rebirth. Still the mania did not stop, forcing me to my knees again and again, but hope returned faster. The last episode occurred in 2006 and I have been in solid recovery ever since.

A Tough Grace

For several reasons I had a harder time with this illness than many. There were eight adverse drug reactions in all, plus a ninth that put me in the hospital to discover that two beta blockers were needed to calm the anxiety from a regular haldol injection. The other reason I had such a hard time is that I lived alone. There was no close family. Thus, there was no one to see my early symptoms, or to give me feedback or to take action to get me committed. I often took off in my vehicle, traveling to some ten states in all. When I did, the episodes sometimes ran on for months, and I created terrible predicaments both near and far from home. I was hospitalized some 13-14 times in places such as Arizona, Minnesota, North Dakota, Iowa and Wisconsin.

Maybe I took some very rough hits so that I'd be forced to plumb the depths of manic depression, forced to dig hard for the meaning and healing modes in order to bring back a new view of mental illness. I constantly sought new forms of healing so that I'm now a small encyclopedia about some 50 methods and approaches. The illness, however, needed to run its course in order to experience the underlying pattern of wholeness beneath the chaos. But it has been a bone-crushing path. I feel lucky to have survived. By all accounts I should be dead by now.

The net result, however, is that I know myself as few people do. I've been pushed to my limits so many times that my knees are scarred, but my story is also full of miracles, lessons and gifts. I say today that I would not have wanted to become the person I was becoming before this illness. Manic depression, with all its tortuous ways, has been a profound spiritual path.

Alice A. Holstein

A Tough Grace

To be forced to undergo a journey through the wilderness is an archetypal experience. Perhaps everyone who is called to a higher psycho- logical development must undergo such a wilder- ness experience....Looked at purely clinically, the journey through the wilderness appears to be a sickness or breakdown; looked at spiritually, it may be an initiation or rite-of-passage we must undergo in order that a change in consciousness may be brought about. Egocentricity dies hard in most of us. Often only the pain of the wilderness journey can bring about the desired new attitude.

John Sanford
The Man Who Wrestled With God, p.22

Chapter 2: Honoring Suffering and the Hero's Journey

The first inkling that there might be something valuable about the suffering came when I relocated in 2002 to my home town, La Crosse, WI after 40 years absence. There I came into contact with the Franciscan Sisters of Perpetual Adoration (FSPA). No one connected with them said anything in particular about honoring suffering initially. Perhaps I just sensed it because of their strong social justice ethic. Or maybe it was their knowledge of the saints and mystics and the suffering many of them endured. Their compassionate stance was demonstrated by their ability to listen non-judgmentally. Speaking the truth about my path, only some of which I tentatively shared, was possible in these circumstances. This helped me begin to stop living the lies that hide mental illness. The Sisters were accepting and empathetic.

Alice A. Holstein

Participating in a spiritual direction group led by one of the Sisters paved the way to seeking her out after a manic episode when I was having trouble integrating psychotic aspects of the experience. Feeling otherwise fearful about sharing with others who might be judgmental, I found her receptiveness to be therapeutic. Then I found the mysticism series offered at the Spirituality Center. This reinforced the ties between mysticism and manic depression. Hildegard de Bengen, for example, experienced years of visions before she found the strength to act on her convictions through writing and lectures to priests and Bishops about the ill effects of the patriarchy. Before her emergence into a tireless life of education and service work, however, she had taken to her bed with illness. She spent ten years writing her first work. As the Franciscan Sister who gave this program suggested, there is a very thin line between mysticism and mental illness. Joseph Campbell similarly compared the life of the artist and the mystic, finding their lives very parallel. He suggested that the artist with a craft remains in touch with the world while the mystic frequently spins off and loses touch. (Cousineau, 1990)

The mysticism series later gave me the courage to share a paper I'd written with the Franciscan Sister. Its theme was about how suffering provides invaluable wisdom. As William Styron, the writer who suffered a debilitating depression in his 60s said, "suffering is an opening to wisdom." This was the first time I had linked the two concepts in writing.

In the fall of 2004, as the Sister and I were discussing the ties between mysticism and manic depression, she introduced me to Wayne Teasdale's work. One chapter of his book, *A Monk in the World,* is devoted to his bout of cancer and what it taught him about suffering:

A Tough Grace

Suffering provides us with lessons that dispose us more
readily to divine union and helps us to consider those
things we take for granted. Tough grace puts these
things in front of our face. We are pushed to make
decisions about our relationship with God. Tough grace
brings about a radical simplification of our lives by
purifying our hidden motives with love and compassion.
It high-lights just what we need for the spiritual journey
and counsels us to leave the rest behind. In this way
tough grace is itself a gift, though it may be the kind of
gift we aren't too anxious to receive, until we witness its
profound transformative effects on us. Then we
understand.

(Teasdale, 2002)

From the Baha'i faith comes a similar understanding -
that "in every suffering one can find a meaning and
wisdom." But it is not always easy to find the secret of
that wisdom. It is sometimes only when all our suffering
has passed that we become aware of its usefulness.
"What man considers evil turns often to be a cause of
infinite blessings." (Abdul'l-Baha, undated.)
    Gradually I was re-framing my suffering to see it
as a purifying experience. Finding a tape by Carolyn
Myss, author and international workshop leader, called
"Spiritual Madness" revolutionized my thinking. In it she
said that spirituality is usually portrayed as sweet and
easy and this is not to be discounted, but that it is often
filled instead with hardship, pain and suffering. There
we are tested and tried. There are taught things
such as humility, surrender, endurance, compassion
and facing all our fears. I listened and listened and
listened and took notes from that tape - and healed
several more notches because I identified so much.
    As I interacted with some of the Franciscan
sisters, and as I found these readings, I began to wish

wistfully that someone had helped me claim suffering in a positive sense earlier, had helped me hold it in a way that would have made me feel better about myself, less judgmental and more patient. Nowhere else, however, such as the treatment system, did I find any hints that suffering might be valued. Instead, both professionals and others conveyed the attitude that "ain't it awful" you have this illness and do such damaging things. If anything, the fact that I was attempting to honor suffering in myself was dismissed. Perhaps it was misinterpreted as feeling sorry for myself, or a glorification of suffering that is not helpful either. Somewhere in the middle, however, there is a balance where suffering can be appreciated for its role in building character and spiritual growth.

Finding this kind of value in suffering also carries with it a profound respect and empathy for the suffering of humanity. Never again will I see a homeless person, a drunk, a mentally ill person or anyone hurting with the judgment I once possessed. Not one of us escapes this human condition, whether from loss of loved ones, war, illness, natural disasters, disabilities, financial woes or the hardships of poverty. Suffering is universal. We have only to look around the corner or across the room to find someone with heavier burdens or simply those that are particular to them. But let there be no doubt that the mentally ill suffer greatly, mostly silently in a world that often treats them as less than human. Oftentimes the suffering is so severe that people die unnecessarily. Why, then, can't we better honor suffering's presence in our lives and turn a compassionate face to it? To do so helps people find the storehouse of life lessons beneath the pain. To honor suffering can be profoundly life-giving and healing.

The Hero's Journey

The Hero's journey of *separation, initiation and return* frames a revolutionary view of manic depression, but I didn't realize the deeper application of Joseph Campbell's work to the illness until late in my journey. Since the 1970s, however, I had been collecting information about how various authors, thinkers and fields named the stages of growth that must be navigated if people are to become mature human beings. More than 30 expert opinions, Campbell's included, show a similar path of growth stages that typify the route to higher consciousness. This is communal proof that humans are on a path of evolution beyond the egocentric state of the patriarchy. The applications to mental illness are definitive. There *are* stages of growth beyond normal egocentricity, and manic depression can be a way to achieve them. Psychiatry lacks this knowledge and consequently it cannot see the possibility that mental illness can be a profound spiritual path.

Bill Moyer's interviews with Campbell made his work popular through the PBS television series, *The Power of Myth.* The journey is marked by suffering, resurrection and rebirth. The experiences can apply to younger years, mid-life transitions and many situations where people are tested and tried in extraordinary ways. The younger years are most often when manic depression surfaces, so Campbell's words about this transition deserve special attention.

He describes the puberty or initiation rituals of tribal societies where the child undergoes psychological transformation, giving up their childhood thoughts and behavior to become an adult. The passage is from psychological immaturity and dependence to the courage and renewal of self-responsibility as a young adult. A death and resurrection is required. This is the basic motif of the universal hero's journey; having to suffer before you find a new sense of life and meaning. (Campbell, 1988.) Campbell identified such transitions as a universal condition, yet popular culture barely knows about it at whatever age it occurs. When they do, they see it as abnormal versus common. Some religious traditions, however, recognize this crossing point; many Native American tribes still hold rituals, including sending their young people out on vision quests, but for the most part we are void of this myth and its relevance to various stages in life. Some of us are called to several cycles of this journey. Those who suffer with manic depression could proudly claim it as their path.

My most profound insights from Campbell's work came from his *Mythos* video series. In it he relates the Navaho legend about "changing woman" and two traveling boys as a typical hero quest myth. The story, in brief, recounts the travels of two boys who must complete a series of tasks, fighting unbelievable battles in order to survive. Nonetheless, they receive help of various kinds along the way. Their journey takes them around the world to the end of its known boundary, meaning they leave the direction and norms of the larger community. The hero must leave behind this known territory in order to bring back totally new discoveries. Along the way they are forced to pay a price to gain the rewards. The dangers in the Native American myth include extreme tests. If the boys were not worthy of their travels they wouldn't survive.

One task was to go to the central mountain to slay the monster that was troubling their mother. Another was to encounter "big lonesome monster", a creature that spit them out four times as they became exhausted. Their survival, however, was aided by receiving magical help.

A Tough Grace

Through the details of this typical mythic account of leaving the bounds of the world in which you've been brought up, Campbell illustrated what it means to go beyond all that is known. This is the story of the creative person, a characteristic often associated with manic depression. True autonomy and strength to challenge the status quo are the result. To follow this inner directed path, he said, involves danger and darkness versus the more practical outer-directed path followed by the majority of the population. On this lesser-known path, one that is still relatively unknown in modern society, people travel in the domains of transcendence to acquire what is missing in society.

The hero's journey is one of death to one's little ego and finding the illumination that is beyond good and evil. In the process we come to know our inner selves, becoming capable of unique gifts. The manic depression experience, however, is one where the person enters the abyss of darkness and too often does not find a way back. The way we are treated, the drugs we are given and the way we are labeled inhibit or prevent a safe return. I would guess that nearly all of us who suffer have no idea that our path may be part of a heroic journey.

Nowhere are we exposed to this kind of guiding myth; seldom are we encouraged to tell our stories; never are we told that underneath the outward symptoms of battle, fatigue and non-acceptance might be an underlying search for wholeness. The opposite is the case. We are seen as damaged goods, often treated according to negative labels, rejection and dehumanization. Both the illness itself and these reactions cripple us. I submit that the reason we do not find our way back is that we do not know how to re-frame our experiences as Campbell does.

The details about this mythic hero's journey, although I had known about it in general before, gave me a tremendous boost beyond the negative definitions and conditions that had so thoroughly penetrated my own self-definition for most of twelve horrifying years. His tapes validated my journey of exhaustion and being dismembered. It affirmed the abyss of darkness into which I had fallen and the wasteland through which I traveled. It explained some of the magical help I had received, realizing only later that I had been supported all along the path. It also affirmed my return as a taller, stronger person with my own story to share. The positive impact of this re-framing was extraordinary after years of shame and stigma.

Such a guiding myth is totally absent from the field of medicine and mental health. These systems, in fact, represent the boundaries of the known world. Tragically, for both them and us, too few of us are equipped to fight the battles and bear the burdens that accompany this heroic path. Instead, we allow ourselves to be judged by others' standards, to become beaten down by them, rather than having a picture of an alternate route to wholeness. Such a path requires far more effort than the one required of more practical "normal" humans.

The larger issue behind this lack of myth and meaning is that our whole civilization has lost its center. The combination of a lost civilization and the lack of a guiding hero myth create an unbearable burden for the person suffering from manic depression. As Campbell says, the failure to become centered and whole again thus robs us of creativity, artists, poets, writers, musicians, true health and life itself. (1996)

It is difficult enough to deal solely with the symptoms of trauma without the added anxiety of knowing why we are experiencing them or whether they will ever ease. Anxiety can crop up for a variety of reasons, including a deep pain that comes when your spouse, friends and relatives unite in the conviction that it's time for you to get on with your life. They want you to act normally because they believe you should have learned to live with your symptoms by now. There are feelings of hopelessness, futility and despair that accompany being incorrectly advised that the only way your symptoms can be alleviated is through a lifelong regime of medication or therapy.

Peter Levine
Waking the Tiger (p. 46)

Chapter 3: Hidden Causes of Manic Depression

The doctors told me constantly, "we do not know the true causes of this illness."
They see it as a disease of the brain, often with a genetic link. What they do not see is all the things that affect the brain, such as diet, beliefs, energy healing, etc. Once in a while a doctor would ask me about my childhood, but so much of this information is suppressed that a superficial question misses the mark. We do not know what the suppressed memories might be without the help of alternative healers or guides. I had already discovered considerable family dysfunction during my mid-life transition, but the mental illness would push me deeper to understanding its depths. One book written from the traditional medical viewpoint at least stated that there is often a correlation between the illness and early

loss experience. The reference, however, meant the loss of a parent or significant care giver through death. Physical loss had not been the case for me, but other losses were significant and equally disabling. I was loaded with unresolved grief.

This idea that manic depression is merely a brain disease to be treated mostly with chemical solutions takes us down a blind alley. It causes researchers to look for answers only in our genes or in the constant emphasis on drugs. Unfortunately, even the Supreme Court has declared that it is a disease-based illness of the brain. The National Association of the Mentally Ill (NAMI) made a similar declaration, one which reinforces for both sufferers and their families the idea that nothing can be done about it except to seek medications treatment. The point here is not that mental illness is not a brain disease but rather, that manic depression *is* a brain disease that also usually omits the factors that influence the brain. Once in a while I heard or read the suggestion that traditional psychotherapy might be helpful, but the cost made it prohibitive. The doctors did not push it, knowing how impractical it was.

There is sound evidence nonetheless that other treatment modes are available, but they are mostly alternative ones and must be supplemental to conventional treatment. Candace Pert, a Ph.D. pharmacologist, who did cutting edge research about the relationship between emotions and the body (*The Molecules of Emotion*) found that emotions come not just from the brain. Rather, they are found throughout the body. As a practical matter this means that emotional events or trauma from the past are stored at every level of our nervous system and even on the cellular level. The unconscious mind has a profound influence on psychosomatic illness, happiness and wellness. To me this means that alternative modes must be utilized to heal the trauma. Most body workers know that emotions become lodged in the cells of our body. Our issues are in our tissues. They proceed on that assumption, seeking the blocked energy flows and the suppressed experiences that are the cause of so much illness. "Body work is such a powerful healing art that it can facilitate a process whereby the recipient can get in touch with their feelings and bring about a healing of mind, body, heart and spirit to be set free!" (Glassey, 2010)

Pert's work has profound implications for seeing and treating mental illness. Her scientific conclusions demand that alternative complements be considered and used far more widely than at present. Such possibilities presently lie outside the traditional medical model and the mental health system in general.

My experiences suggest that there are multiple causes for the illness, different by degree in everyone who suffers. The pieces fell together in 2003 as I was reading a nutrition and diet cookbook, *The PH Factor*. There were many passages about mood swings inherent in the chemical make-up of our bodies, which can be treated with diet. They even suggested that our DNA can be altered by this approach. The brain is one of the most sensitive organs nutritionally in the body.

Suddenly I saw the total picture. My earlier abuse of alcohol, my earlier addiction to smoking and my earlier poor dietary habits could be related to the illness. They are all related to chemical changes in the body. As soon as I began to eat differently, I felt better. The fact that smoking depletes us of critical vitamins was something I had read about years ago. The same is true for alcohol, but the doctors seldom address this or other things that might affect brain chemistry, such as beliefs, imagery, music, energy work and more. The only reference to food I heard during the twelve years of my hellish struggle was to "eat a healthy diet." There was no further guidance. Drug usage is also a huge precursor of mental illness.

Personal verification of the link between diet and mood swings came from my stint with a naturopathic doctor. He did a complete blood workup that included information about vitamin deficiencies and other key elements, like copper and zinc. His approach reinforced the relationship of illness to alcohol, smoking and diet. My work with him did not "cure" my illness, but it made a significant difference to how I coped with it.

Many manic depression sufferers use alcohol to self-medicate; they often smoke to stimulate themselves or to deal with anxiety while suffering the effects of medications. They often eat poorly from ignorance or the lack of money to buy the right food. A friend of mind, for example, relied upon public food pantry handouts. Starch and sugar are plentiful from these sources. As soon as he began to eat properly with my help, he felt better immediately. His system cleared and he had more energy and mental clarity.

I too felt the positive effects from the naturopathic doctor's regime, which did *not* include taking me off psychiatric medications. In 2002, however, I suffered a serious bout of side-effects from lithium despite standard blood tests to watch for overdose symptoms. I suspect the side-effects occurred because I had worked so diligently on balancing my physical body. The healthier you become, the less you are able to tolerate toxic substances. Psychiatric drugs are often just that. Severe diarrhea and vomiting occurred, probably throwing the drugs out of my system and thereby triggering mania. I didn't know at the time that these side-effects are traditional ones associated with lithium. This is still another case of poor doctoring when you are not informed about potential side effects.

I didn't know either at that point how ultra-sensitive I was to medications. Many years passed before I stopped being so dependent upon the doctor's standard, by-the-book dosage. It took me years to become an advocate for myself. I had to become adamant about my ultra-sensitivity, which nonetheless was often not heard despite such declarations.

Beyond this insight about the role of physical imbalances in contributing to manic depression, I believe that the most important causes are ones that are mostly outside the traditional medical model's purview. They are usually out of our own conscious awareness too. These principal causes come from emotional wounding in our background as well as the culture at large; they also come from spiritual or creative openings that occur while we are internally unbalanced enough not to be able to handle them. The two factors are related. When we are wounded within ourselves from trauma, which manifests bodily as blocked energy as per Candace Pert's work, then we can't withstand the creative forces that bombard us.

A personal example of the effects of trauma comes from a "big dream" I had in 2002. The dream said that I had abandonment issues and needed cranio-sacral help. How can a dream be so specific? I do not know, but it was one of the miracles I received, for it had profound healing effects. I realized, over a three-day period of cascading reflections, how abandonment had been so strong in my background. I could trace the beginnings of my mood swings to the mid-1980's when my parents seriously rejected me for talking back to my father during a family business crisis. He proceeded to disinherit me for a brief time for such a challenge and my mother followed suit. Since I had no children and only a limited support system, the loss of my family was a serious emotional blow. I had not realized how serious it was until that 2002 dream opened the floodgates.

There were other abandonment incidents that surfaced, from lovers who left to my beloved mentor when I fell in love with a man who met with her severe disapproval. Most importantly, as I continued to dig for healing insights and emotional-physical healing from 2002 onwards, I verified that emotional wounding played a large part in my illness. These were suppressed memories that only body work or other innovative methods would reveal. There was sexual molestation plus World War II atrocities that my father likely participated in that I unconsciously lived out as a victim. This is called wartime "survivor effects." There were the losses not grieved that characterized my mother's life, resulting in her lack of presence to me as a mirroring mother. There was the physical punishment meted out to me, the littlest one in the family, by a father who displaced his anger with my mother onto me. She, in turn, felt abandoned by him when he went to war when he was old enough not to have to go. She never forgave him for it. Later he made me partly his companion. I had a love-hate relationship with him. My mother lived her life through her children as a stereotypical homemaker. All of this family baggage means I was often, unconsciously, the parent to the parents. This is a classic set-up for depression. I also know that I am emotionally an ultra-sensitive person. Things that might roll off other people hit me hard.

In terms of emotional wounding, the feminine energy has been abandoned in our culture in general. Both women and men have suffered this wound. Our masculine-dominant, scientific-rational society negates feelings, the inner life, the darkness and the slower, softer pace of the feminine energy. It emphasizes doing over being, achievement over relationships, possessions and principles over love. We are an unbalanced, still patriarchal culture.

A Tough Grace

There is a relationship between emotional wounding and spiritual openings.

Before my medical diagnosis in 1995, my mood swings took on the nature of spiritual insight and creativity. I had mystical experiences; I had creative visions. But these experiences began affecting me in mood swings that I couldn't handle because I was still disembodied or ungrounded. The swings moved from creativity to psychotic in 1995, the year of my diagnosis. Now, I believe that I was chemically unbalanced, suffering heavily from emotional wounds in my body. And then there were the hormonal changes of mid-life as well as the chemical imbalances from alcohol, smoking and poor diet. The combination was nearly lethal.

But what about the prevalence of manic depression in young people? Could this be spiritual too? The fact that a spiritual opening might contribute to triggering manic depression at younger ages is verified from several sources. The illness is most often diagnosed in the teens or early 20s, although my mid-life diagnosis followed a not uncommon secondary pattern according to one doctor. Young people frequently experience a spiritual opening in early adulthood, as already mentioned by Joseph Campbell. Native Americans too recognize this passage. Youth is a time of significant stress for young people seeking their place in the world. Seldom are they helped to do so through ritual or the emotional support involved in transition. Elisabeth Kubler Ross was another who suggested that spiritual openings often occur in young people. She proposed, during one of her workshops I attended in 1985, that such experiences and the advent of a far more creative life than usual would be common if our rationalist, achievement-oriented culture did not prohibit this. Jungian Marion Woodman also endorsed the concept of spiritual light first arriving at a young age. Other Jungians do too, suggesting that this is the beginning of a meaningful life that only later bears fruition if we do our inner mid-life work well.

Almost all doctors and mental health professionals, however, label these spiritual breakthroughs as being crazy, the result of delusions of grandeur or hallucinations. Add to this the use of drugs by some young people and you have a stew of trouble. Mystics and saints, however, frequently indicate that one must be extremely healthy in body and mind to handle such input. They most often were supported in their journey by cloister or monastery, places that provided emotional and physical support. How I wish that I had had such support to help weather the storms. As it was, I had spiritual openings and I glimpsed the higher reaches of human nature. I felt a supernatural energy and consciousness. I tapped these levels, but I also slipped into psychosis and madness. There were multiple causes of my illness.

Energy healer and medical intuitive, Caroline Myss, believes that many modern-day mystics are emerging, traveling the path without benefit of community or economic support. They also do so while living out the disconnection from nature, the mind-body split of civilization in general. Myss suggests that "spiritual madness" is the defining spiritual path, not the one characterized as some sweet, easy route to enlightenment as we usually think. Instead, it requires courage, endurance, hardship and suffering, all of which cleanse us of old roles, behaviors and attitudes.

Psychiatry and the mental health system would do well to investigate these multiple causes. They are difficult to discover, difficult to quantify, difficult to treat, but their acceptance as part of the journey to wholeness would do wonders for our ability to heal. Right now clients are too often passively dependent upon only medication. At the very least, we should be educated about the multiple causes if not steered to appropriate alternative help that could be undertaken with safeguards. It is not that one alternative method or the other is the answer. Rather, it is a case of healing at physical, mental, emotional, spiritual and social levels. Many methods may be necessary, or at least should be available to personal choice. This multiple-cause and multiple treatment approach could provide hope and healing for millions.

Alice A. Holstein

I learned that struggle tempers the steel of the soul. It straightens the backbone and purifies the heart. It makes demands on us that change us forever and make us new. It shows us who we are. Then we make choices, maybe for the first time in life, that determine not only what we'll do in life but what kind of person we'll be for the rest of it.

Sister Joan Chittister
Scarred By Struggle p.85

Chapter 4: Losses and Grief

A photograph of me from 2001 shows a body blown up like a balloon. I gained 55 pounds over the weight of 165 that I carried before my diagnosis in 1995. Given an allowance for some weight gained as I aged, the major cause of this poundage was psychiatric medications. Zyprexa, with known, significant weight effects, was the worst offender. I gained 30 pounds in several months. My eating was out of control. I felt helpless to do anything about that, nor was I told that this could happen. Lithium is another known offender. Both of them were part of my medication "cocktail " that a doctor once told me was the crapshoot they were forced to play to get the right combination for each person.

The corresponding loss of an acceptable body image with its effects on self-esteem is one of the many losses that the mentally ill suffer. Doctors often just shrug their shoulders, suggesting that side effects are a necessary evil.

There were severe financial losses. My life is half a million dollars less from out-of-pocket medical expenses, clean-up costs, spending sprees, lost income and reduced social security benefits that will plague me for the rest of my life. This may be a conservative estimate. There is another half million spent by others for hospital bills, disability benefits and taxes I never paid. Fortunately, I was not reduced to poverty, but many who suffer manic depression do end up there. Some barely exist on disability benefits because of their limited ability to work, whether from interruptive behavior or just feeling so lousy that they cannot work. This means that we live with economic dread, losing the freedom to feel confident about our financial future. We also fear never being well again. Besides losing a significant income, I lost a career as an organization consultant, college teacher and author; I lost self-esteem and the structure in daily life that working provides. I lost dignity and hope. I lost physical strength, and I almost lost my rights as an ordinary citizen through threatened institutionalization. I lost my mind during mania; I lost coherence and the ability to think during and after an episode. I lost the ability to make sound decisions or the ability to make decisions at all during depressions.

One of the hardest losses to bear was the loss of friends, family and colleagues. Part of this is understandable. Some people fear the mentally ill and their sometimes disruptive behavior. Fear and lack of understanding keeps them from empathetic response or extending the helping hand to re-establish support and community. We thus lose the very things that would help us cope better in recovery - the company of companions who are healthy and could give us the acceptance we crave. The loss of dignity and self-worth, the existence of labels and stigma is hard to bear. We usually suffer in silence. When support mechanisms are provided, such as halfway houses or drop-in centers, we are limited to those of our kind.

Being with other people with similar or worse problems can be helpful, but they don't always make for a cheerful, uplifting atmosphere. Thus, I tended to isolate myself rather than experience outright shunning. I suffered the mortification of knowing what my public, sick behavior had been.

Besides losing friends and colleagues, I allowed family relationships to lapse because of the illness. I lost face and faith in myself. Temporarily I lost the will to live, although suicide was never an issue because I decided in my college years that that option was unacceptable. I did, however, beg God time and time again to take me because I was so exhausted, so bereft from fighting the battle. I denied myself the ability to buy tickets to movies and concerts, clothes and eating out in order to buy alternative healing. I had more resources than most, but I lived an austere life.

Another thing I lost for a number of years was the security of knowing I could care for myself as I aged. Seeing the resources drain at an alarming rate, feeling unable to work, meant that I lost hope to be very productive again. I lived in fear of having to live a subsistence existence. I regularly also lost possessions and belongings. Sometimes this was the result of messes I created, sometimes from frenzied cleaning states, sometimes from things I damaged during a manic episode. Several times I lost the ability to eat on a regular basis, or to eat healthy food. I lost the ability to cook for myself, periodically, when I lived as a homeless person. Most horrifying of all, I sometimes lost the ability to keep myself clean. And I lost a sense of safety as I lived on the streets. During the worst of my delusions I thought that I had actually lost everything because I believed I would not survive.

Ask anyone with a serious illness or who has become disabled and they will say that losing one's health is the hardest loss to bear. I lost it for twelve years; many lose it for the rest of their lives. I am still fragile in a way I was not before, but I am lucky to have regained my strength in general. I am not "cured" in a final sense, although my daily existence has improved drastically compared with what it once was. There is still a loss from facing that I am sentenced to a lifetime of medications. I hate to be dependent upon pills. I wonder about their long-term effects on my body.

Losing the core of ones being, which comes from having a fractured self, is a state that others cannot see and do not understand because they have never been so disrupted. After an episode, however, we are largely left on our own to put ourselves back together again, to somehow just get on with life. We do not wear bandages, use crutches or sit in wheelchairs; we cannot claim heart attack or cancer that bring get well cards, sympathy and acceptable absences from work. Seriously injured people may be helped to know that they must die to an old self and rebirth a new one, but such understanding is not extended to the mentally ill. We look "normal" on the outside, but we may be hemorrhaging on the inside, never quite dealing with the psychic pain that comes from so many angles. So many times I felt that I never had the chance to really recover from the last manic episode, and I feared the unspoken terms, "psycho, nut case, deranged, sick in the head, irrational or crazy." Our condition is labeled most commonly as "bipolar mood disorder," inviting constant negative reinforcement. Who would want to be labeled "disordered" even if you have been that way repeated times? We are almost never free of the battering that comes from being diagnosed and labeled as damaged goods. The term, mentally ill, has connotations like no other illness, and it is a loss to our Self to hear and know that.

Some mentally ill people lose their lives from the bone-crushing load that losses and other trauma incite.

A Tough Grace

Many families lose money, hope and freedom from inexplicable behavior of a loved one too. They lose hope for a better future; families are often torn asunder in the process. There is a stupefying accumulation of loss, both financially and otherwise, for millions who suffer mental illness and those who share their sphere.

Despite my multiple losses, the deepest pain was the loss of my potential. To know myself as a once creative person, to have the feeling underneath that I had so much to contribute, to believe I had an unsung song inside me was the severest blow. I had to surrender to that truth many times, which wasn't entirely bad. I had to find the will within to be ready to do whatever I could, however small, to live a life of service and contribution. This is a type of surrender that helps rid us of egocentricity. To have emerged from such darkness, to begin to sing that song, however, is now accompanied by humble, joyful gratitude. I want to make a difference in other lives, and I finally have that chance. My mind works well again; my will to live and give is strong once more.

The pile of losses we suffer need to be grieved and let go of, yet we remain untreated for them by doctors and the mental health system that is detached except through some counselors who can be helpful. Good case workers can be important too. The grief can come out partially in some support groups. And I found several healers with whom to shed my tears. I learned to cry regularly, whether from despair or because of the losses. I did forgiveness exercises; I found or made up my own grief methods and rituals to empty my load. There may still be unshed tears, more work to do to heal the trauma that comes from manic depression. During these years of recovery I needed to do some crying for myself because all of it has been so unbelievably hard.

Post Traumatic Stress Syndrome (PTSD) has become the well-known soldier illness of our time. Its frequency is alarming. The phenomenon, however, is seldom treated in people who suffer from manic depression or schizophrenia. For those of us who have not been in wartime combat, there is a kind of wartime that some of us know well. This comes from the trauma of psych wards, the clean-up messes, from dehumanizing treatment and chronic stress, from flashbacks that can haunt us by day and by night. Some of my behavior was so interruptive that I suffered with deep mortification about what I had done or said. I also identify with the PTSD of wartime survivors and their families, mostly from my illness and partly because I am a Vietnam-era veteran who initially suppressed the effects of being an intelligence officer while briefing B-52 pilots flying combat missions during that war.

I have healed a great deal of the manic memories, but not all. There are still embarrassing thoughts, painful reminders that surface from time to time. One time I was so loaded with them that I took myself to a bed and breakfast southeast of Tucson, Arizona for five days. There I spent several hours each morning using the upper body acupressure tapping approach of Emotional Freedom Technique (EFT) to tap my way through hundreds of incidents. (See Chapter 8, "Search for Healing.") I felt lighter afterwards. I can't remember now what I tapped away, which suggests that incidents from the early years are mostly gone.

Another approach I used was to read about PTSD in general, including sources that identify how easily trauma is embedded. Authors such as Peter Levine, Judith Lewis Herman, Stephanie Mines and Alice Miller all testify to the prevalence of trauma in the psyche. As I said earlier in this book, I believe that unhealed trauma is a major cause of manic depression. We simply do not know how easily it is incurred. Reading these authors and coming to understand trauma was another important part of my *re-framing* process, legitimizing the pain. The search also encouraged me to pursue deep healing methods such as energy work, Family Constellation workshops (See Chapter 8: "The Search for Healing") and more. Through all of these approaches I learned that the power of insight to heal is overlooked. I didn't become aware of all these untreated aspects of loss and trauma until 2006 when I realized with a rush how alone most of us are with this load.

Alice A. Holstein

Don't be afraid to crawl inside and wait. To do less until direction comes. To make a decision not to make a decision. To promise yourself nothing but the hurt until the hurt heals. Let the deep hurt, hurt you deeply until it releases you.

Marguerite Reiss
Holy Nudges, p. 91

Chapter 5: Psychiatric Wards and Doctors

In some ways I had a harder time with this illness than others. In other ways I had it easier. I was older when diagnosed, had successful work experiences and life skills. I was used to living and coping alone; I had a higher education, loaded with a strong psychology background based upon knowledge of the healthy human being. My research and writing skills swung back into use when I began to reclaim my life in earnest in 2002. I had enough resources to avoid poverty, and I had done my mid-life inner work so thoroughly that this center of self held amidst extreme chaos.

In addition, for nine years before my diagnosis I had the love of my mentor and beloved friend, Elizabeth, which fortified me for the long run. I also had a few friends who stayed the course with me through thick and thin. Miracles blessed my path. My independent spirit, stubbornness and a seeking nature stood me in good stead. Thus, I was blessed with uncommon resources to weather the storm. Some storms, however, came from a faulty medical model in a faulty health care system peopled by a few professionals who should have been fired for inhumane treatment.

Psychiatric wards have been life-saving places for me when I was a danger to myself or others. Thirteen or fourteen times I was confined to one in various locations. Some 18 psychiatrists crossed my path, about six of them helpful in one way or another, although all except one were wedded to the traditional medical model. Thus, they were extremely limited in how they viewed potential healing.

The wards provided locked doors to keep me safe, treatment for my demons and sometimes simply the place where I could be taken care of while I slept. I needed to recover from the worst of an episode until I regained the courage to face the outside world again. They were almost always, however, traumatic places to be. I rate them in my mind as bad, medium and good, but none were excellent. My ideas about enlightened treatment include recommendations that hospitals be much less relied upon than at present. They are terribly expensive ways to treat this illness; their therapy programs are limited and their atmospheres are not necessarily conducive to healing. They are stop gaps that provide little transition to much needed aftercare.

A ward in western Arizona was one of the worst I experienced. I made the mistake of asking the doctor about his experience and qualifications. His answer was that he had been trained in an offshore medical school. He was arrogant, cold and indifferent. During a Chapter 51 hearing, which is the legal term for a legal, involuntary commitment process, he ridiculed me for some of my bizarre behavior. The lawyer sent to represent me arrived for the first time 15 minutes before the hearing. Before she came, during the long wait for help, I was consumed with anxiety about what might happen as a result of the hearing. Would my rights be suspended longer than a few days? How would I cope then? The doctor threatened me with long-term institutionalization, and I was in despair. Finally I was rescued by a social worker who intervened to make arrangements with my Tucson doctor to receive me there as a patient upon return. This was only my second confinement for the illness. When you are new to "the system," away from home, you not only feel isolated as a sick, crazy person - you feel terrorized about what others can and often do try to do to you.

Because I was escorted home across the state in a Sheriff's car, I had to leave my car behind for later retrieval. The doctor would not allow me to drive, although the Tucson doctor decided after two day observation that I was in good shape. The earlier treatment had included several nights of being forced to sleep with the lights on in my room. There was never any explanation about this preposterous order. Group therapy beyond a mediocre crafts group was missing. The only saving grace to the experience was that the State of Arizona footed the bill; that social worker in the system had saved my life.

In North Dakota I was subjected to another arrogant doctor who lacked any consultative skills at all. He kept me heavily drugged for days. Their treatment consisted of video tapes that were shallow and unhelpful. Attendance was mandatory. I otherwise slept most of the time from both exhaustion and the drug overdoses. I had not learned yet how to be an advocate for myself, but it would have made no difference. The doctor won our control battle hands down. There is extreme anxiety and despair when one is held captive by incompetent people.

By comparison, a hospital in Thief River Falls, Minnesota was a treat. I stayed for three days of evaluation after being picked up in a commercial laundry for some bizarre behavior, including parking my truck in someone else's garage. The hospital treatment brought me a psychologist who explained the medication options and their side effects. Only one other doctor out of those 18 had done the same. Usually you are prescribed without consultation or explanation. Thief River Falls also had some excellent therapeutic tapes and several groups that kept me occupied for three days. Then they decided that I needed no further treatment. Their staff was friendly and helpful. The Chaplain was a welcome source of support. Whenever I asked to see a Chaplain in a psych ward, it was almost always a comfort. Usually you have to ask for such help; the medical staff generally does not realize what kind words can mean, regardless of your religious choices.

Several visits to a psych ward in my hometown terrorized me because of an authoritarian doctor who didn't listen and used threat. The first time I encountered him he didn't ask at all about my history with adverse drug reactions. The prescription for Depakote later gave so many debilitating side effects that it was one of those times when I thought I could not bear the illness. He gave me no education about these possible effects, but I subsequently learned from some nurses that they were common. Afterwards I fled to an alternative healer who felt like a life-saver through both her treatments and her medicine woman type wisdom. The non-judgmental attitudes and refined energy of alternative healers may be as important as their methods. The doctor-patient relationship is crucial.

But this doctor had a horrible bedside manner and was known to be a problem in the hospital. He threatened me with a six month stay in the state mental hospital. Again, I was in despair for several days, wondering how I could cope with this fate if it became reality. Since I lived alone at the time, my life would have completely fallen apart for lack of being able to handle my affairs. I was bereft. Only the intervention of my case worker and the promise of her being responsible for close follow-up saved the day.

A Tough Grace

An even worse scenario unfolded the second time I was exposed to this man. He again threatened me with institutionalization. He testified to that in my Chapter 51 hearing, having never read the staff case notes about my remarkable recovery over the previous five days. Upon admittance, he had put me in isolation for 36 hours without explanation. There was no doubt that I was disturbed and disturbing to others upon admittance, but the lack of communication from anyone about why I was being isolated was terrorizing. Even a crazy person can be reached with kind words about what is being done to them and why. I was also forced to eat alone in the hallway during this period. I was humiliated and frightened. I was not violent; I had no suicidal tendencies. The room I occupied had no shower, and I was allowed nothing except some scraps of paper, a pencil and a Bible. No one bothered to tell me that I could have been "let out" briefly to take a shower under supervision. When you are already isolated from your "normal self," such treatment raises the sense of paranoia and isolation to decibel level.

When I tried to secure a different doctor, I was blocked at every turn. My lawyer, however, decided to have me testify on my own behalf and I was able to make a case against this psychiatrist. The judge declared the doctor-patient relationship irretrievably broken, but by then it was too late. I had already been victimized. Most of that stay was spent documenting when and how my rights had been violated, seeking redress from an unresponsive patient advocate system. That program was a joke. Even after speaking to a representative and thoroughly documenting the problems, no one did anything or followed up. When I spoke to the psych ward manager about this situation, she twice promised to get back to me later. She never did. Mentally ill patients don't count. They can be ignored at will. She apparently felt no need to provide the courtesy to minimally respond.

Stories about this doctor were common on the ward; he reduced some people to tears, and even the staff clucked sympathetically about his behavior. They could understand my frustration and despair, but they were helpless to do anything because the doctors in the system rule supreme. I consider that his treatment extended my stay by at least three to four days, but the bill was mine to pay for service that was frightening and dehumanizing. Several other visits to this hospital were far better. Their therapy programs, while leaving much to be desired, were some of the better ones I've experienced. There is little incentive, however, for staff to pursue knowledge that would address the depths of our illnesses, including alcohol and drug abuse that count for many of their admissions. Hospitals are mostly temporary depositories, resting places and drug dispensers.

A hospital in Iowa was another terrorizing place. After a Chapter 51 hearing during which my lawyer indicated I would not be forcibly injected, I was confronted with exactly that a few hours later by a security guard and two unkind nurses. I was not dangerous at all, but they menacingly threatened force unless I cooperated. My anger erupted afterwards as I threw my hands in the air and marched out of the room. This only created more trouble. (Later, upon return home, I would suffer a severe reaction to the injection ordered, which had been administered not only with threatened force but without explanation.) Why can't a doctor or a nurse tell you why something is being done? It is not enough to say that it is the doctor's order, who by the way is absent during this travesty. It is assaulting and inhumane to be treated this way.

. My anger produced the order for isolation; waving my hands in the air, which was not done threateningly, was judged to be dangerous. To me it was justifiable objection to the injection. While in isolation I was not notified of meal times, devoid of television and drugged very heavily. The weekend doctor accidentally revealed that I actually could move about although I was expected to sleep in isolation. I spent most of the 14 days there sleeping because the doctor would not listen when I spoke up about my medication ultra-sensitivity. There is no choice about taking pills in that situation; you are watched by the nurses as they are downed. Again, I believe these conditions lengthened my stay by at least three to four days. Their therapy programs were mediocre; the nurses were occupied only with paperwork, chit chat among themselves and little interaction with the patients. Therapeutic listening came only from a few nurse trainees from a local college. During all of my hospitalizations, I can remember only a few professionals who employed good listening. Several of them, who displayed it when I was in despair, remain gratefully emblazoned in my memory. Medical professionals have no idea how life-saving can be the act of merely being listened to and valued.

It would be a long time before I recovered from such treatment. In 1992 I had published a book about the rigorous inner work required by the mid-life transition. (Mack, *Beyond Turmoil: A Guide Through Deep Personal Change*). Although such knowledge about life passages is somewhat commonplace in the culture, especially in Jungian literature, it appears not to have penetrated the medical model at all. Despite the book and my substantial expertise in humanistic and transpersonal psychology, I did not fully recover my faith in this background until 2006 when I felt like Rip Van Winkle waking up from a dozen years of lapse and painful naps. Only then did my fight to go beyond the medical paradigm lead me, finally, back to the core ideas in my book about a whole person concept of a physical, mental, emotional and spiritual being needed, and that required healing on all these fronts.

At the present time psych wards are essential for treating mental illness. They too often, however, contribute to the trauma we incur from other factors. Just being diagnosed with labels, being locked up, being treated as though we are invisible or without sensitive emotions is hard to bear. Sometimes it makes us distraught almost beyond repair. I still feel like a battered woman to have endured the attitudes and behavior encountered in psych wards. Sadly, I conclude that medicine has done me great harm. It has taken a long time to restore my self-esteem and sometimes I feel as though it is permanently scarred. I do not believe hospitals are the only options for treatment, and the uncalled-for experiences in at least half of them where I resided were unconscionable.

This brings us to the next paradox of entering into the kingdom of God; it is those who have recognized that they have been injured or hurt in some way in life who are most apt to come into the kingdom. There is no virtue in our weakness or injury as such, especially if this leads to self-pity, which completely defeats the creative purposes of the kingdom. But only a person who has recognized his or her own need, even despair, is ready for the kingdom; those who feel they are self-sufficient, those whom life has upheld in their one-sided orientation, remain caught in their egocentricity.

John Sanford
The Kingdom Within, p.49

Chapter 6: Pilgrimages To Faith

Some of the clearest if not best memories of my sojourn come from living as a homeless person for some six to eight months of my twelve years. They became the best recollections because there were so many defining moments when I learned, upon reflection, who I really was - how I coped, what I endured, the miracles that blessed my path and what I experienced to deepen my compassion for all who suffer cruelly in the world. I say that I lived *as* a homeless person because I still had financial assets, including a home I'd hurriedly left in Arizona, propelled by paranoia and the episode that followed the lithium poisoning. Although I had assets, I was too paranoid to tap them or got separated from cash or credit. I often thought that all was lost. I may have had financial resources, and sometimes I knew it, but just as often I thought they were gone forever.

For a long time I bought the "ain't it awful" opinion about my escapades. Some of the incidents are, indeed, still difficult to accept, but for the most part I have *re-framed* them to view them as pilgrimages. As Shirley MacLaine points out in her book, *Camino: A Journey of Spirit,* being helpless and vulnerable is what pilgrimages should be about. She walked nearly 500 miles across northern Spain along a well known pilgrimage path, the Camino de Santiago, trod by spiritual seekers since ancient times. Carrying a bare minimum of supplies and a walking stick, she encountered hardship after hardship that transformed her life. The book had been recommended by an energy healer after she heard about my cross-country trek from Arizona to Wisconsin.

I had never heard this definition of pilgrimage before, but gradually I saw my
hair-raising trip in a new light. There had been unbelievable hardship, including crossing a wide river laced with both ice and bitterly cold water. During this manic episode there were hills on the other side of the road, open highway ahead and fear of what lay behind me. There was no choice, it seemed, except to cross the river, aiming for another part of Colorado Springs that lay in the distance. Alternately, as I confronted the ice and water I took off my shoes to navigate the shallow, frigid water with my shoes tied around my neck. Then I put them back on to walk over more ice. I still don't know how I forded this river, nor do I remember how long it took. I was on foot totally by then because my car had been towed after I'd parked it in the lot of an apartment complex with the keys locked inside.

Once on the other side of the river, I walked until I found an empty classroom building where I used a restroom and calmly sat down to rest, shivering, before the police picked me up. Snow was beginning to fall as they escorted me to the Salvation Army shelter.

A Tough Grace

At the shelter I slept on a canvas, stained cot, ate in a dingy dining room and cleaned up in a room where two of four showers were not working. Holes in the walls of the building had been punched without being repaired. My stay there only lasted several days; my paranoia caused me to flee.

A snowstorm was in gear when I left, wearing only Oxfords to combat the wet and ice. I had to be crazy to leave, and I was. The next shelter was a battered women's facility. I had to lie to get in, saying I had no ID when I actually did. Still a heavy woman then, I had to heave my cumbersome body up a bunk bed ladder, tumbling in exhausted but grateful for the sleep and warmth. The dorm-like room with a few bedrooms branching off from it was full of crying children sleeping on the floor. Women got the beds, and the last one had been issued to me.

Another time in Colorado Springs I was driven to a soup kitchen by a cab driver who gave me a free ride. The kitchen had opened for emergency sleeping when the temperature fell below freezing. We slept on thin, gray pallets on the floor, so close together that you had to be careful not to disturb your neighbor if you turned over. They issued one army blanket per person, but hearty food was available the next day at the crowded picnic tables. There were no showers, merely old style bathrooms. I used my shoes for a pillow, covering up further with a few clothes that I wore in layers. After the soup kitchen closed its doors when the weather improved, I slept in several cardboard boxes nearby. Whenever I was in those situations, I slept near the lights of a place for safety. It is a miracle not to have been assaulted.

Another time I sheltered near a door where some warm steam issued forth, camping out with a family that was also homeless. I slept on the cement that night, not the last of my cement beds. In

Minneapolis one time I hid underneath a basement stairwell for eight days, existing only on bread and water. After drifting in and out of sleep for several days, I returned to a more normal schedule of waking, then sneaking upstairs at night to use a restroom where I washed my hair with hand soap and otherwise cleaned up. My mind was occupied by writing notes on tiny scraps of paper. I "wrote" some of a book in my head, realizing then that I should write it sooner rather than later. Eventually a hospital guard found me, kindly ushering me out without calling the police. A bus driver gave me a ride downtown. I carried my plastic bags as usual. Such was the state of being a genuine bag lady, toting slim layers of clothing and the meager possessions of survival.

There were many nights spent sleeping in open fields, using black garbage bags for protection on the ground, wrapping my feet and arms in them, sometimes sleeping on porches out of the wind and cold until the owners might wake up. I slept behind bushes, in ditches, on park benches. One night I woke up on the cold steel of a playground merry-go-round, having knocked myself unconscious when I slipped, bumping against the rails while trying to get up on it to escape some thoroughly wet ground. After that I slept, sitting up, on a bench outside a store with another homeless man who told me about the shelters nearby that we didn't use. Snow and sleet fell before us.

During 2003, in Minneapolis, I found another battered women's shelter with only one other woman occupant. My bed was a couch, which felt like pure luxury, but there was no shower. Eventually the episode led to a hospital where a social worker issued me a $26 bus ticket home. Although I was relatively clean underneath, my dirty, smelly clothes mortified me during the trip. Sometimes, when the clothing layers couldn't be switched any more, I found bathroom spray deodorizers to douse the clothes. People must have wondered about such perfumed scents wafting down the street.

One time in Colorado Springs I walked for six days without eating, careful to keep myself hydrated. The hunger went away after several days. My clothes began to feel baggy. 40 pounds were dropped during my four month trek to La Crosse. Many nights I was forced to walk all night; it was the only way to keep warm and remain halfway safe. I was often exhausted, wondering how I could go any further. When I didn't have to walk all night, my survival tactic was to cry myself to sleep. This meant really sobbing, but it was purposeful. With such purging I found I could get up and go for another eight-twelve hours the next day.

These are but a flavor of the experiences when I found myself homeless, too paranoid and helpless to act rationally. The events and places blur, but these times are also when most of the miracles occurred. (See the next chapter.) During these and other times, I was picked up by the police at least half a dozen times, then escorted to a shelter or a hospital where I was committed. One time, early in my illness, I fled out the back door of my condo as the commitment team knocked at the locked door. Crashing through the desert cacti and brush, I hid until nightfall, then slept in a dry ravine. The next morning I made my way to a complex where I rented an apartment. Later there was an eviction because the paranoia led me to run away again rather than stay there in the safety I'd established. My finances had become so tangled that I couldn't manage my affairs, despite the fact that there was money in a nearby bank. Similar events created some horrible clean-up messes that had to be endured long after an episode had run its course.

Also in Colorado Springs I checked into a Bed and Breakfast, leaving without paying. Desperation overcame me because I was sick with a bad cold and had to have some rest in a warm place. Another time it was the Edgewater Hotel in Madison, WI where I walked away without paying. I always sent these places a check after sanity had returned. Knowing that lying sometimes seemed necessary to survive was painful because integrity was so important to me. I was desperate when I did. The actions were prompted, irrationally, by the feeling that I was not safe anywhere that a "normal" person might seek help. The police were all corrupted and so were organizations in general. Designated homeless shelters felt more unsafe than other places because of drugs and the people they attracted.

After being hospitalized in La Crosse, at the tail end of my four month trek across country, I suffered a near death experience. For three days I was absolutely certain that death was coming soon. This was not unreasonable, given the fact that I had been so long without my thyroid medication, a life-threatening condition. Such deficits can also severely worsen a manic episode. An elderly Franciscan sister at St. Rose convent "saved" me by merely listening to my despair without judgment or advice. Facing death was not fearful since I had faced it so many times before, but this was one of the times when I was virtually inconsolable about leaving the world without making my contributions. The Sister's listening grace gave me the strength to go the next steps forward, but not before I made out a handwritten will and sent it, along with my diamond rings buried in a pair of socks, to a friend in Arizona whom I requested to be my estate executor.

Not much later, as I started over in La Crosse, it felt as though rebirth was occurring, step by miraculous step into a new life, guided through every need by more and more miracles of finding just the right place and just the right possessions on a limited budget. Since there was great uncertainty about when my home in Arizona would sell or the exact state of my finances, frugality was essential.

Sometimes during these homeless periods I had cash or credit; sometimes I had nothing except what I found for food or shelter along the way. Sometimes I was able to get to a place where I could get or resume tapping my assets, but I was delusional and paranoid a good deal of the time. The details remain fuzzy except for these defining moments that I later *re-framed* as a colossal series of pilgrimages in various parts of the country.

Several times I "lost" my car either to being towed or because of crazed behavior or else had left it in an airport parking lot, so I rode Greyhound buses with great delight. I slept on them; I read on them; I wrote on them and straightened out my life as best I could until the next stop. I also lost valuable possessions by storing things I couldn't carry in their lockers. Earlier, in Colorado Springs, a van load of valuables was lost, including gift items for that mysterious organization staff I was supposed to assemble to help transform the world. After the van was repossessed, the company that handled the car's contents, Allied Recovery, lied about how long there was to recover the items. They said a week, but I later learned it was a month. Ford Motor Credit, which hired the company, was no help either. They stonewalled me. These are examples of how the mentally ill are taken advantage of. A lawyer's intervention when I was sane, trying to resurrect the damage, brought no results except insults from the company. The legal fees still needed to be paid, but the lawyers should have told me in the beginning that my case was hopeless.

Everything in that vehicle was gone forever, including irreplaceable family pictures, jewelry and clothes and other prized possessions. Many of my important documents had to be replaced. The clean-up cost about $40,000. Various other clean-up situations meant a huge loss of resources plus guilty feelings because I was otherwise a careful money manager. I watched the financial resources drain with fear. And the acts and their traumatic consequences were mortifying.

Only later could I re-frame these incidents as a series of pilgrimages that led me on a journey toward faith. Claiming my warrior's badge freely, I realized how consistently I had been cared for by acts large and small. Despite hunger and deprivation, the next thing or person that kept me going was always provided. Serious hardship and physical pain were my lot, but I had not been harmed physically by anyone. Instead there were countless examples of tough grace. Later reflection showed me that a rock-solid faith had become firmly anchored. The outcome of the near death was to initiate a rebirth process that would be tested many times before I stood safely on solid ground, but what I ultimately saw was that I had been a pilgrim who learned indelible lessons to help transform my life.

During the most difficult moments, especially while coming across country, my only companion was a God who sometimes seemed only cruel. I railed at this force and cried a lot. I felt abandoned, but he/she or they, as I later called them, were ultimately protective and caring. My union with them was palpable. I saw them later as both female and male. My God was now an androgynous force, the Yin and Yang of the universe, the Alpha and Omega, the soul and spirit, however you want to name them. This presence was life-saving during many episodes. I frequently give thanks now for having my life saved amidst so much despair and danger. These pilgrimages were not accomplished alone. Often "God" came in the form of "little people" who will never know that their acts of kindness and love kept me alive to tell this story.

A Tough Grace

I wish I had their names to acknowledge them in this book. As another friend says frequently, "everything we do in life counts." I know the truth of that many times over. The smallest encounter, the simplest word or expression can make another's day. Such things can also save a life. Mine was saved literally hundreds of times, whether physical or psychological, during these twelve years. The hardships added up to pilgrimages to faith. These incidents alone are enough to define my journey as a profound spiritual path.

Alice A. Holstein

A Tough Grace

The Lord is close to the brokenhearted He saves those whose spirits have been crushed.

Psalm 34:18
International Children's Bible, 1988

Chapter 7: Miracles

The dollar bill was inserted in the door crack of my 1993 Ford Ranger truck when I left the library one afternoon in 2005. Looking around to see if anyone was near, I sensed immediately that it was another tangible miracle. Just the day before, after visiting my caseworker to assess my progress, I had told her that some day there would be a story to tell. Imagining myself standing before an audience, I envisioned starting a talk by holding up a dollar bill to suggest that they were looking at a million dollar illness personified. The bill represented the $500,000 that it had personally cost me plus another $500,000 from others that included some hospitals that paid the bill, all the caseworker and police/court services, the government's disability support and their lost income from taxes I didn't pay. My costs included back-breaking medical bills, lost income, spending sprees, messes to clean up and reduced social security benefits that will plague me for the rest of my life. Indeed, the million dollar estimate may be conservative. The talk that I would give to various audiences would end by holding up another telling symbol - a bathroom deodorizer can.

The can, of course, would stand for the way to overcome smelly clothes during homeless episodes. Except for homeless shelters, there are simply no public places to get clean. I wore layers of clothing that I switched around, plus taking sponge baths in restrooms kept me relatively clean, but the clothes sometimes became too much. These two symbols, the dollar bill and the deodorizer, represented the two ends of my spectrum, from desperation to health. I also envisioned suggesting to an audience that they never knew who might be in front of them when they dealt with someone who seemed destitute. There is a person underneath.

I thought that both symbols might make an impression on an audience. The mystery, however, was how to account for the bill sticking in my truck when only a day earlier I had imagined using it to start a speech. But by this time miracles were not unusual. There had actually been many of them, including tangible objects, people who appeared just in the nick of time, events that saved my life, comments or listening that helped me cope or keep going.

In Colorado Springs, in 2002, running down a highway in winter wearing a skimpy pair of shoes, I came across a pair of sturdy, black Oxfords just my size. They were sitting on the road beside a guard rail on an otherwise deserted stretch of road. Paranoia had sent me running down the road after my car had been towed from that parking lot I've described before. The fact that the shoes had shoelaces was critical to my survival. After stumbling down a steep bank, there was no alternative except to keep going across the river, alternately tying the shoes around my neck to wade through the icy water while putting the shoes back on to walk on the ice.

As I reflect on these miracles now, the story of "the peace pilgrim" comes to mind. She walked without possessions, except for a toothbrush and a small notebook, in total faith that she would be provided everything she needed along the way. That did happen, including food, shoes, shelter and opportunities to speak about peace as she crisscrossed the country for thousands of miles.

A Tough Grace

In La Crosse, Wisconsin, I found a pair of warm, suede gloves on a park bench one evening. The air was bitterly cold, laced by a penetrating chill from the humidity. Was this before or after I found a wind breaker wrapped around a tree in front of an apartment complex? The lightweight jacket was just enough insulation to take my shivers away. That same apartment complex, where I eventually rented a one bedroom apartment as soon as I had restored some finances, yielded still another boon. The former tenant had left me two sets of towels with which to begin my occupancy. The rental agent was perplexed himself, commenting, "Enjoy them. We can't use them otherwise." Since I was seriously exhausted at the time, with no energy to furnish the place or start housekeeping and no car to easily purchase things, this was a huge gift My possessions consisted of a K-Mart lounge mattress, a blanket, my clothes and a coat. The towels, a bare minimum of food, paper and plastic plates and instant coffee, allowed me to sleep 16 hours a day for two weeks while some strength was restored. 2002 marked a new beginning.

Even renting that particular apartment turned out to be wise. Worried about money, at first I'd rented a small, dingy one. When it turned out that the door lock was broken and the tenants left the outer security doors open all night, I beat a hasty retreat to the rental agency to break the lease. Instincts, however, indicated that the apartment complex where I eventually found the towels was the place to begin putting my life back together again. I was used to being guided by such hunches, but I didn't discover until later why this place made so much sense. This complex was virtually the only one in town that allowed me to break my lease if the purchase of a home was involved. After four months in the apartment, my Arizona townhouse sold, so I knew where I stood financially and could afford to buy a modest condo in La Crosse.

The requirement from my Chapter 51 hearing in May 2002 stipulated staying in La Crosse for 90 days. At first I was bereft. How could the Arizona house sale be handled? Then came the idea to hire my friend's husband to execute the move, including arranging for the packing and the moving van. That arrangement was a Godsend, for return to the southwest would have been impossibly exhausting. Recovery from the cross country odyssey took months; it was even more draining to move from the one bedroom apartment to the new condo. So often there were events like this. At first they seemed like disasters, but later it was clear that there was some benefit or purpose to it all.

Similarly, having my van repossessed in Colorado Springs - not for lack of payments but for staying too long in the tow yard - had initially seemed like a disaster. The news that it had been repossessed came one day after it was done, too late to prevent the event. I had delayed attending to the mail while other priorities were solved. There was nothing I could do except wince about the car. The financial loss was tremendous, but the event also freed me from hefty car payments and from the need to pick the van up when I was so seriously debilitated. Using the local bus system was a bonus while I was getting back on my feet. Doing so was fun; you see things on the bus that are otherwise missed when driving a car. There were people with whom to have chatty conversations and the drivers were friendly, all of which helped me feel less isolated as I slowly returned to living life instead of merely existing.

There had been other miracles in Colorado Springs. One time a woman and her two teenage children took me to a hospital when I was hyper-ventilating from fear and cold. They stayed with me while I was treated and regained some composure.

A Tough Grace

Then there was the Congregational church outreach worker who gave me $20 to get to a homeless shelter. While there, sitting on the thin sleeping mat, a woman came up to me one morning with a pair of thick-soled tennis shoes. There had been no request for help. With the biggest smile imaginable, she said simply, "Here, honey, maybe you could use these." By this time my black Oxfords had seen better days. That woman's gesture and smile still shine in my heart, bringing tears to my eyes. So many things like this meant so much along my route when I was grasping for straws.

Before that van was lost, there had been a man in Pueblo, Colorado who saved me from being picked up by a police force that he indicated would not be very friendly. He had noticed me acting strangely as I went in and out of a convenience store while my car was parked at a gas pump. Coming to the car window to warn me about the police, he literally begged me to follow him to his apartment. Many would say that my acceptance of the offer was dangerous, but I had survived on gut instinct in so many situations already that I trusted my reactions. I followed him to his apartment. Having money at the time, I bought the pizza we shared while he told me a little about his life as a newly divorced man and how hard it was to adjust. Then he gave me an afghan and blanket for the couch. The apartment was askew; obviously this was a bachelor unused to living alone, but safety there felt assured. Unfortunately, I left before he awoke and lost his name and address. He was truly a kind savior.

Another time, in Los Angeles, a Christian couple who took me in for a week said they simply believed in helping others. At the tail end of an episode that had not involved hospitalization, I nonetheless had no money or identification. I found myself at their house after leaving a rental car at a shopping mall where I'd pulled in to its lighted parking lot to sleep. Sleep deprivation was upon me after driving in circles on the California freeways. Rest was essential. While there, something or someone spooked me, causing me to leave the vehicle while I walked all night. Later we discovered that I had walked 15 miles without shoes. What saved me was a double pair of socks, one of which was very thick. My purse was locked in the car, but it didn't make much difference, for I couldn't find my way back to it in the morning. I cried most of the way along the route, later ending up at a house where a man was outside doing yard work. Somehow a conversation was started; one thing led to another and soon they offered a room for a week, during which we made periodic trips to nearby shopping malls to try to find that car. We never dreamed that we should search a 15 mile radius.

Another miracle about these caring people was that my management and organization consulting skills proved helpful to them with their cottage industry sweatshirt enterprise. Later I invited them to Tucson to facilitate the development of a business plan that restored their communication and focus. Before they came, while I was still their guest, we finally found the car and soon I was on my way home to Tucson where I could again begin to straighten out my life. This couple was a pair of miracle angels.

In 2003, in Minneapolis, I was in a commercial laundry calling a woman's shelter for a reservation with the last change I possessed. I had no other money. Moments earlier, while picking stray socks out of a basket of discarded ones to use as mittens, a man gave me a $20 bill. I had not asked him for help. His gift bought me a taxi ride to the shelter. Another miracle angel was a holistic dentist who also did bodywork energy treatments. As he was doing a session with me, he mentioned the Hellinger Family Constellation workshop that weekend in La Crosse. (See Chapter 8:

"Search for Healing") When I hesitated about the cost, he said he would forego his fee as a contribution if I wanted to attend. I accepted the offer. Two hours later I was in that workshop, one of several of this type that produced healing breakthroughs. The moment of his offer is crystal clear in my mind; this open door appeared as a special gift and the opportunity would not come again. There were many such moments that required instantaneous decisions. I was in need in some way; the means appeared and I took it.

Other people and their kindness provided many miracles. At times my caseworker, Mary Speltz, literally saved my life by being so available with her sound advice and support. One time I was so broken by the deluge of medical bills after still more episodes that the situation made me think that continuing was unbearable. My back was physically breaking. She had the right support. Mary did that several times for one thing or another, listening to me, urging me on, providing essential resources. Another moment that remains crystal clear is the woman doctor at a La Crosse hospital who comforted me at a crucial moment. That time I had lost my purse at the airport; total despair wracked me because an episode was underway and here I was in the hospital. How could I possibly face doing something about everything that goes with losing one's identity and money? Already traumatized by the episode, confined to the starkest part of the psych ward where you are watched constantly, I was exhausted and terribly broken once again. She put her hand on mine, comforting me with her compassion long enough to restore me. Later the purse was returned to me after the airport turned it over to the police. This was a case of another Samaritan who turned it in at the terminal.

A woman minister in La Crosse visited me in several hospitals and endured some phone calls from far off places when there was no one else to care.

Three friends, Wanda, Barbara and Dree inTucson, Arizona comforted me at key points. The list goes on - Dorothy Wetterlin, a stellar friend, plus a hospital nurse who merely listened compassionately when I was in utter despair about the authoritarian doctor and his threats. Later, during another episode, another nurse just listened while I poured out my story. This triggered some of my initial writing efforts. Then there was the reassuring ambulance attendant who enveloped me in a beaming smile, full of compassion and concern, as we sped through the wasteland of North Dakota.

Another remarkable incident took place in Warroad, Minnesota, where I landed during a snowstorm at a motel at 3:00 a.m. The hour was so late at night partly because there had been no places to stay along the way. Three stops at towns on the way yielded no vacancies. Bitter cold and snow laced the air. While checking into the Super 8 motel, a man arrived five minutes behind me, also seeking a room, but the last one available had been rented to me. While I was there, the steering vector on my truck went out. Had I been forced to go on the night before, I would have been on a bleak stretch of road, broken down in the early morning hours. Luckily a garage down the street was open the next morning, a Saturday. Staying the weekend allowed much needed sleep. As I was checking out the next morning, chatting with the desk clerk about the Native American paintings on the wall, the young manager came out from his desk. He was Native American, and we struck up an animated conversation. That communication with someone with so much presence helped bring me back to reality. I'd been out of touch with people in any meaningful way for days.

More conversations with him took place several days later. He opened up about some of his own trauma; I was a good listener, inviting his trust. He also described his attitude about his life and tribe, his place in life at the moment. It was obvious that he was firmly anchored in his tribe, and his dedication to the earth that his father had instilled in childhood. As I drove back to Wisconsin after encountering this exceptional young man, I felt as though I had made a friend. Furthermore, the lesson I learned from him was that I desperately needed community to anchor me too. I then declared La Crosse as my "reservation" and began the task of creating real roots almost immediately upon return.

The encounter also inspired a return to reading Native American literature, including their healing rituals. One of the authors was Dr. Carl Hammerschlag, a progressive psychiatrist who began to function outside the traditional medical model after being awakened to its shortcomings while working with the Indians in New Mexico. I was reinforced about my search for unconventional healing by reading his books. I was also affirmed by his response to a paper I'd written about my healing journey. He gave me key encouragement to support these initial stabs at writing. My path was graced by one door after another opening to yield further insight and support.

The Minnesota venture was ironic; the town where I'd landed was "Warroad" (war road). I'd been on that path with the battle of mental illness, but I was starting to come home in some bigger ways to safety and breakthrough. The dangers of that trip also sent me scurrying to my next alternative healer, a shaman practitioner. Later he would lead me through a rebirthing session, soul retrieval and a drumming event. His reverent healing attitude and listening skills were the most remarkable of anyone I encountered along my path. There were many times when my desperation drove me to seek the next healing rung on the ladder.

Being saved from physical death was another miracle. On my way home from a less traumatic episode than usual, I was on the Mississippi river road when it was raining. The weather was cold, but the pavement was not slick until a patch of black ice came up from nowhere. Suddenly I lost control of the truck, spinning once around completely, skittering over the middle line, ending up in a snow bank facing the wrong way on the highway. The rear of the truck was in the line of oncoming traffic. Within the space of the next five minutes, six other vehicles hit the same ice. One car ended up just opposite me, a serious accident with a woman pinned inside. Several more cars ended up in a minor crash just down the road. A semi also slithered and jackknifed over the median but remained upright. A man coming toward me in a four wheel SUV careened wildly before coming to a stop several car lengths in front of me. I froze in terror as I heard and watched all of them, wondering when the next one might plow into me, stuck there on the embankment. The noises were like a whoosh with each impact sounding like cannon balls going off. Nobody did hit me in that vulnerable spot. However the man in the SUV, after calling 911 about the serious accident, pulled me out with his tow bar and a rope. Looking down, I saw that I was eight inches from crashing down a steep hill that would have put me onto the railroad tracks below. The chances are good that I would have died or been seriously injured. I didn't start shaking until I got home. And then I shook for a long time in relief and moments relived. It was another miracle.

The larger lesson from all of these incidents is that I was unbelievably protected and guided at so many crucial moments. My only explanation for these miracles is that I was given magical help to survive, just as had the two brothers in Campbell's Native American mythos story. (See Chapter 2: Honoring Suffering and the Hero's Journey.) Somehow I was chosen for some unbelievable trials.   Somehow I was saved over and over again.   Like the pilgrimages in the last chapter, these miracles too make my mental illness a profound spiritual path.

Alice A. Holstein

One tries everything (in order to heal) and nothing seems to work; then a level of frustration arises that is so great that it breaks down the entire system. It is at this point that a radical change of meaning can occur. Such a change can never be brought about by an act of will. It involves opening up to something greater.

David Bohm, interview with Don Factor
Infinite Potential, p. 319

Chapter 8: Search for Healing

Beginning in 1998, with only a pin prick of belief that I could be better, I began a nine year search for healing. I found some 50 methods, practices or approaches which are listed in this chapter. The attitude of the doctors had been gloomy, inviting a sense of hopelessness. Their conclusion was that this illness had to be endured while living at a pretty dysfunctional level. They said that the only solution was powerful medications that had potent side effects, such as dulling my mind, considerable weight gain and sometimes feeling outright sickened. In 2004 I was told by a doctor that this business of finding "the right cocktail" for each person was a crapshoot. Another doctor said that because of my ultra-sensitivity to drugs I was considered in the 2% with the illness who are difficult to treat.

These messages of doom made me angry. I vowed then that I would become as well as possible. Over the succeeding nine years I tried alternative healing methods, individual practices, spiritual approaches and group activities. Some were extremely effective, some moderately so and some were questionable. All, however, were indicative of the will to get better. This *intention* was tremendously important. This kept hope alive. This strengthened my resolve. Even in the darkest hours, the will I had set in motion meant that doors continually opened because I was actively seeking help; the intention fortified me, often at the subconscious level, to get up again and again. The work I did contributed to breakthroughs. Doctors such as Bernie Siegel and Carl Simonton affirmed that one's attitude and self-help imagery affect wellness. Often they determine whether we survive serious illness or not. Siegel even suggests that "the difficult patient," the one who challenges the doctors and takes responsibility for their healing, is the one who gets well.

The medical doctors negated alternative healing efforts. Several were visibly upset that I would try these avenues; one berated me for it. The solution was not to share this side of my search with the professionals. An effective argument to doctors, however, comes from Dr. Michael Lerner of the Commonweal Institute in California. He said he had asked a group of oncologists what made the difference in patient's survival. They replied that it was 1) quality of life, and 2) their functional status, meaning better able to cope. Lerner suggested to them that these characteristics were exactly what were produced by various spiritual, psychological, nutritional and physical approaches that survivors used. Why would doctors deny these to their patients when there was proof that they made a difference?

My question is the same. A caution, however, is that alternative approaches may be unwise if one of them becomes the sole means pursued. Over-reliance can be harmful. Since mine was totally a self-help project and there was no one with whom to discuss things, and since I was terribly discouraged about medications, I used poor judgment several times. My inability to tolerate some eight different medications caused me to give up on them. One doctor replied that he could offer no alternatives. Some insisted that I would just have to grin and bear the side effects. Finally I found the right meds and "the right" doctor late in my journey.

What I did to get well ran the gamut. They included some 50 things, several of which will be explained in greater depth.

Journaling

Naturopathy to balance my body with food supplements and diet.

Mindfulness practices with a group that meditated together, doing walking meditations combined with support for one another.

Attending lectures that highlighted alternative healing approaches.

Herbal treatments with a Chinese medicine practitioner. Healing Circles at an alternative church.

Emotional Freedom Technique (EFT).

Medical intuitive and Swiss energy healer.

Japanese energy healing.

Cranio-sacral therapy.

Healing group based on beliefs and meditation.

Prayer.

Group spiritual direction.

Reiki circles.

Group meditation.

DBSA support group (Depression Bipolar Support Association).

Depression Anonymous support group.

Informal healing group that included hands on healing and support.

A medicine woman.

Acupuncture.

Myo-facial healing, a form of bodywork energy healing. Zone (foot) therapy, a Swedish healing approach.

Hellinger Family Constellation Workshops.

Inspirational/educational videos, such as Joseph Campbell and Wayne Dyer.

Extensive reading in fields mostly beyond psychiatry. Forgiveness practices.

Concentrated work on my diet.

Self-designed grief work.

Shaman practitioner.

Rebirthing.

Exercise (swimming, walking, fitness center).

A Tough Grace

Walking the mandala, a circular maze.

Dream work.

Lectures on mysticism.

Conferences (several, such as "Spirituality Reflected" and Hellinger).

Music.

Specific research on PTSD.

Self-help exercises from Deepak Chopra and other material.

Self-designed rituals.

Affirmations.

Gratitude exercises.

Writing articles or book manuscript drafts to clarify and integrate my thinking.

Collecting significant research that fortified the development of a new view of mental illness and healing methods.

Reading meditative material.

Caseworker counseling over several years.

Hospital therapy groups.

Drumming circle.

Support Circle diagram.

Inspirational/educational audio tapes.

Massage.

Below are some more in-depth explanations:

Support Groups

Even before I vowed to do everything I could to heal, a support group sponsored by DBSA, the Depression Bipolar Support Association, was critical to my survival. The Tucson, Arizona chapter was effectively run by people who suffered from various mental illnesses, from depression to manic depression and personality disorder. Early on, in my periods of psychosis, I felt horribly shamed by the spending sprees and terrible messes I created. At the support group there were horror stories from others about their spending sprees. I knew I was not alone. Other support groups helped deal with debilitating depressions. Several times I could barely function. The only positive thing possible was to crawl to those bi-monthly meetings. It helped to voice my pain, as well as gain courage from others who had hit bottom and climbed out. The group leadership was inspiring if not heroic.

In 2002 the DBSA group in my hometown was also a brief life-saver although it wasn't well run and soon petered out. From 2003 onwards I have periodically attended a 12 Step Depression Anonymous group and still attend. It is a circle of support, a place to speak my truth, to be accountable, to be inspired and to share my own inspiring story. You immediately find acceptance and support in such circles. One of the curious things is that medical doctors seldom know about these community resources or recommend them.

Chemical Body Balancing

Seeing a Chinese medicine practitioner and taking his herbal remedies was the beginning of several attempts to balance my body. Since manic depression is caused by chemical imbalances, this makes enormous sense. It made even more sense after realizing that smoking, poor diet and alcohol abuse could be affected by balancing the body. I did not stop taking the psychiatric drugs during this work.

The most effective intervention was with a naturopathic doctor who was also a chiropractor. After the blood analysis, we began with a food supplement and dietary regime, gradually eliminating supplements as the balances occurred. He muscle tested me on a regular basis to see what supplements were no longer needed. I also did several fasts of short duration under his supervision to cleanse my system.

As the supplements took hold and then decreased, I began to feel better. That was a powerful indication that this was an effective approach. The medical doctors usually asked about alcohol use, but I had quit drinking by the time the psychotic episodes began. There is a 60% correlation, however, between excess drinking and manic depression. This is often more than an addiction; it is an attempt at self-medication to either get high from depression or else to come down from mania. There are many people with dual diagnoses, yet alcoholism is seldom treated effectively as part of the illness, nor is it treated effectively elsewhere either. Recidivism rates are high.

When I was paying close attention to diet, learning to cook differently took priority. A main reference was *The PH Miracle,* proposing that disease begins in our inner environment and that an acidic one promotes it. Their approach, heavily oriented to vegetables, soy, selected nuts and seed and selected grains, is somewhat drastic, but my first trial in 2003 made me feel better as did my second attempt. Later in my journey I worked with a nutritionist with good results from a somewhat different approach. The subject of nutrition remains virtually untouched by medicine; even hospital food is laden with starch and sugar. During one hospitalization, there was a feeble attempt at a 45 minute nutrition class, but it was a simplistic approach to the standard food pyramid. Only four of us, from a ward of 12-15 attended this class.

Energy Healing

I am at a loss to explain how energy healing works; often it is combined with bodywork. Explanations of Reiki, which is one of its forms, pronounce that it is a process of moving universal life energy to support natural healing processes. My search for healing included several methods of energy healing, but one of them stands out. Pam Radosen shares much of the credit for my wellness. She is an eclectic healer in La Crosse who combines energy healing, Emotional Freedom Technique (EFT), Shamanism, talk therapy and more. Her work helped me get in touch with trauma that went back centuries in my family, plus I worked through many other issues that were blocking wholeness and health.

Bodywork

One of the most effective tools I found was an incredibly simple acupressure tapping procedure that broke a serious depression and later helped deal with a load of Post Traumatic Stress Disorder (PTSD). Called Emotional Freedom Technique (EFT), it involves tapping key acupressure points on the upper body that are tapped in sequence after initiating the process with an acknowledgment of the issue troubling you. (i.e. "Even though I am feeling depressed, I love and accept myself.") Note that the process begins with a feeling or an issue, versus stuffing it as we often do, then an affirmation that helps counter the negative self-talk that plague the mentally ill.

Learning to do this takes a brief coaching session, plus some reinforcement, but it is a self-applied process that is available thereafter for free! There is abundant Internet information available, including its medical origins and how to find coaches in your area. Some can teach you on the telephone. My introduction to the process was one of those doors that opened suddenly after a lecture on alternative healing techniques where I was introduced to Mary Stafford in Tucson. She generously gave me an initial private session for free and then a fee break for a weekend session conducted to train potential coaches. Some relief came in the first session, and by the time the weekend was over I felt virtually free of my debilitating depression.

The process is amazingly simple to use, but tends to be discounted because of this and its practically nonexistent cost. The real benefit comes from starting with the issue, then completing additional rounds that lead you deeper into other feelings or issues. This, in turn, takes you still deeper so that both physical relief and insight are achieved. Apparently it has been therapeutic for all kinds of health issues. This makes sense when we consider that stress is a factor in illness of any kind.

Insight

The fact that insight alone is healing hit me broadside when I was reading physicist David Bohm's biography. The latter section of the book described his battle with depression, including manic depression. Bohm had had discussions with the spiritual teacher, Krishnmurti, about the nature of consciousness and how thought itself functioned. Bohm concluded that there was, indeed, a self, but this self is not an object but an entire mental process, an ongoing activity. "Insight brings about a radical change in the brain, not simply at the level of neural pathways, but right at the quantum level." (Peat, 1997) Several times during 2002 I felt the effects of insight in strong waves. It was as though some electric currents were going off in my head, as though new connections were being made. I felt the same sensation when other rushes of insight came together, such as reading *The PH Factor* that gave me the clues about the multiple causes of the illness. Another example is the "big dream" I had in 2002 that I had "abandonment issues." This insight produced several days of identifying all the times I had been abandoned, tracing my illness to that family rejection already mentioned.

There are many other examples of how insight led to healing. In workshops, such as the Hellinger Constellation work, or through my reading, I found insights that helped me re-frame my experiences, understanding them in unconventional ways. Now I see that it was not just those healing methods that helped me get better; my whole journey to wellness has been a process of gathering education and insights. In addition, powerful people with high consciousness, such as speakers or healers, may well set up a "field" that affects us positively because of their authenticity and being well developed people in general.

Author, Toinnette M. Eugene, in *Women's Spiritual Journey, Women's Lives,* says that positive mental health is related to "command of the environment, self-actualization, self-esteem, integration of the self, autonomy within community and adequate perception of reality." (1995) Most of these factors may be unavailable to the mentally ill, but insight can be a powerful tool if not the most powerful one to help us achieve positive mental health. I developed mine almost in opposition to the prevailing paradigm. The existing treatment system barely recognizes even the value of education. Patients remain dependent, too seldom encouraged to become responsible for their wellness, treated by doctors who think they know it all and who virtually never suggest alternative routes or information outside the traditional medical model. The one exception to this viewpoint is that a powerful grassroots recovery movement is underway.

Hellinger Family Constellation Work

In 2003 I was introduced to Hellinger work, which is one of the most valuable but difficult modes to describe. During a workshop you identify an initial issue you want to work on. This is done without much discussion or lengthy telling of your story as in therapy. When it is your turn to do a constellation (only by choice), you invite other participants to play the roles in your family system. You position them intuitively to reflect the family dynamics. Then the people playing these roles mysteriously pick up the words and body movements that typified the dynamics of many years ago. There are many "aha" breakthrough as this scene unfolds. You see what was really happening in those family relationships, and as the words and movements unfold you find the ring of truth in this picture. Then the facilitator guides some further interactions, using both words and body movements, to heal the broken connections that have impeded the flow of love. Oftentimes dramatic secrets are revealed, such as one suggesting that my father had participated in some atrocities in World War II. These later affected me. This "survivor effect" has only recently been recognized as a factor in succeeding generations. Sometimes the Hellinger work reveals secrets or events that go back several generations. There are often significant emotional releases, such as crying or anger that help dispel unhealed trauma.

The process was developed by Burt Hellinger, a German ex-Catholic priest who observed the importance of family connections in his work with tribes in South Africa. He then immersed himself in various psychotherapy techniques to develop this approach. The work has been used for nearly 30 years and it is especially popular in Europe although it is making inroads in the United States. I think the work is so important that it should be institutionalized in mental health work, at least made available on a voluntary basis. Follow-up after a workshop would be in order. Czech psychiatrist, Stan Grof, suggests there is evidence that the more you work on the underlying problems of mental illness, the more likely it is that it can trigger additional episodes. (Grof, 1980) This seems to have been true for me. For twelve years I kept having episode after episode. Perhaps you become dramatically open at deeper levels that temporarily unbalance the system again.

The Healing Dilemma

How many people are willing to pursue these alternative healing methods? One practitioner, writing about the application of Hellinger work to psychotic illness, provides clues that apply to alternative healing in general. He believes the underlying cause of not pursuing such approaches is the careful keeping of family secrets, affecting grandparents, parents and children. Sometimes it goes even further back. "Initially the elders experience something that creates a traumatic, confusing and schizophrenic situation in the family. Talking about it, however, would be too dangerous for everyone and would endanger the continuity of the family system. Such events, sometimes going back to previous generations, commonly involve incest, love affairs, war, adultery and mysterious deaths. The repression of these events becomes passed on to the children in an unconscious way, reaching them as disassociated feelings and thoughts. The result in the younger generations is delusions and hallucinations. When the secrets are exposed, then the psychotic patient can be released from the psychosis."

Thus, the author of this article has reservations about how many are willing to pursue such truths. Family members who do not want the truth to be uncovered can inhibit or prevent such efforts. "Sometimes whole families will sacrifice themselves rather than expose their secrets. In such cases we must withdraw (from doing Hellinger work) and accept what is. But for those who want to find a good resolution to the threatening past in their family history, we can be of some help in ending this poisonous process of confusion." (Ruppert, 2002) The meaning of his findings is significant. When dealing with mental illness the prevailing attitude is that genetics are at fault and therefore nothing can be done. Professionals and lay people alike also talk about brain diseases without considering what affects the brain. Ruppert's work and others, however, suggest that mental illness, even if genetically linked, may be corrected with this innovative approach. This is truly ground-breaking work that must be explored. Pursuing only chemicals and genes is a blind alley that negates striking new possibilities.

Caroline Myss is another who suggests that we do not heal because we fear change, which upsets life. We sometimes sabotage our own efforts out of this fear, or because we have known our illness so long that it has become part of our identity. John Sanford suggests that the mentally ill may be those readily involved in being flooded with contents of the unconscious, but that the healing of repressed incidents could mean taking on a responsible role in society, such as that of healer, mystic or Shaman. And, as Joseph Campbell writes, the hero's journey is one of potential danger, creativity and privilege which carry the burden of eventually sharing with humankind. Such roles are outside the role of conventional life. They are mostly unknown. Assuming these roles can be a lonely path.

In sum, those who suffer with mental illness have little help to do alternative work. The weight of the whole medical, scientific paradigm and the common perception of mental illness conspire to inhibit the search. But there *are* methods that help heal, some of them potentially significant and many that add up over time. The path, however, requires courage, endurance, persistence and the willingness to be both responsible and different from others who bear these illnesses.

The lack of an accurate and comprehensive diagnostic concept has serious consequences for treatment because the connection between the patient's present symptoms and the traumatic experience is frequently lost. Attempts to fit the patient into the mold of existing diagnostic constructs generally result, at best, in a partial understanding of the problem and a fragmented approach to treatment.

All too commonly chronically traumatized people complain that all their complaints are not well understood. They may collect a virtual pharmacopeia of remedies; one for headaches, another for insomnia, another for anxiety, another for depression. None of these tends to work very well, since the underlying issues of trauma are not addressed. As caregivers tire of these chronically unhappy people who do not seem to improve, the temptation to apply perjorative diagnostic labels can be overwhelming.

Judith Lewis Herman
Trauma and Recovery, p.118-9

Chapter 9: Enlightened Treatment

Changing the face of mental illness, at least manic depression and depression if not other forms, must begin with a new view of its underlying causes, new healing methods and needed structural changes. This is a paradigm shift of immense proportions. With it, however, can come an end to stigma, harmful labels, severe trauma, lack of patient responsibility and wasted lives. The whole society will benefit in numerous ways.

Changing the power structure will be difficult. Medical doctors are invested in the status quo through long years of training in the traditional model. They will have to significantly adapt, undertaking retraining. They are likely to be defensive and resistant. Research, now focused on drugs and genes, will have to be recalibrated. Even institutions, such as government research labs, need to understand that it is not scientific proof of one or the other alternative methods that might be useful. Rather, it is the whole person who needs to get well - physically, mentally, emotionally, spiritually and socially. Who can tell what works and what doesn't, especially when the beliefs of the patients and those who treat them are the most critical ingredients in wellness? If we wait for scientific proof, which is merely the old model dressed in faulty clothes, we will make little progress. The person is holistic despite illness. The healing process must be holistic too. There are innumerable things that can help heal, including love, which cannot be measured.

The drug companies will also likely be resistant. They have billions invested in new drug research and treatment; we are bombarded with advertisements that pills are the solution to everything. The culture as a whole is lazy about or unknowledgeable about the hard work of transforming the inner self that makes such a difference in achieving a creative, meaningful life. Many doctors are in collusion with the drug companies. The fact that these enterprises spend more on marketing than research is a little known fact, covered up with lies to justify the highest medication costs in the world by saying that they need money for research that gives them their return on investment. Hospitals are also invested in the way they currently deal with mental illness, and they are staffed by psychiatrists who operate out of the old model.

State and local mental health systems may be more interested in change. Current treatments are strapping their budgets, but the solution is usually to cut services to the most vulnerable rather than change their own structures. Nonetheless, there is a consumer recovery movement afoot in the field that could be strengthened with a new view of mental illness and the possibility for enlightened treatment. At the present, however, it is a fledgling effort, woefully inadequate.

Revolutionary, top-down change has seldom been the successful way that systems transform. Even mandated legal changes are resisted, leading to more layers of bureaucracy, disgruntled workers and disenfranchised patients. The symptoms of failed systems are treated rather than the underlying causes and symptoms.

While working as an Organization Development consultant, I was trained to believe that top-down change was the place to start. This was essential, said the experts. True, change is difficult without this sanction, but it soon became discouraging to try to push the stone uphill. Too often the changes didn't last; the system reverted to its old ways despite considerable "progress" in the short term. I concluded then that individual transformation, deep personal change, was a critical ingredient to system change. I wrote a book about that, including a chapter, "Beyond Greed and Power: The Giant Ego of Business." I tried to work at that higher level, but that didn't work very well either when wholesale greed took hold in the 1990s. Then I began working on "people's revolution" strategies with my research and author's pen.

The same strategy will likely be necessary in mental health. The consumers are the ones who hold the real power if we will but seize it and become accountable for our own journey and wellness. There are many things we can do to become proactive. (See Chapter 8: Search for Healing) When our attitudes and consciousness change we can become models of transforming our lives. Much of the change is a *re-framing* process. When we change our ideas about something, there can be miracles for everyone. You have no idea of the influence that comes when each of us recognizes and uses the light that everyone carries. Our heroism in the light of severe obstacles is already legendary, even if we are slumping under the weight of the illness or when our efforts remain unacknowledged by others. Ghandi said, "Be the change you want to see." The time to claim this power is now. Chain reactions to others can create hope for us and for mental health in general.

Beyond the fact that doctors may be the last to change, the number of psychologists far outnumbers them. They may be more open to whole person ideas. Nurses are more likely to want to change too. I found many who felt oppressed and disgruntled by having to function within the system. Nurses were better listeners, more empathetic and caring.

The need for therapeutic listening throughout all parts of the treatment system is paramount. It is known as "active listening," which I used in my former career. The skill needs to be a mandatory life skill, starting in the fifth grade in school. Whenever I instilled it in a team, I got comments that it had revolutionized their relationships at work and at home. Until people learned it, they usually talked past one another, falling into strong opinions and arguments. There was considerable inefficiency in communications.

I can count on two hands the number of times I was deeply listened to during my journey. Always, when that happened, I "came back to myself" more quickly: I felt understood and valued. I could let go of some fear, feel restored and able to face everything else with more strength. This is why support groups can be so helpful. The tendency to judge others, to offer advice, is held in abeyance in those places while we speak our truth and listen to other voices.

My recommendation is an insistent one - that mental health staff everywhere, at every level, be required to undergo an active listening class of at least four hours every year, including concentrated practice sessions and shorter refresher courses. These could easily be conducted by existing staff, by someone who has a flair for the subject; the intervention would be low cost and beneficial to internal staff development too. After I realized how life-saving that listening could be, I was amazed at how often caregivers instead used logic, argument and advice when I was clearly illogical at the time. To receive this kind of communication when one is irrational or traumatized only isolates us further from an already isolated psyche. So who are the really illogical ones in this situation?

In the later years of my journey, I became an outspoken advocate for good listening skills. I let people who did listen know how much I appreciated it. I told a number of nurses that they had no idea how helpful and restorative this skill could be. This is feedback they seldom receive, and many of them genuinely want to help.

Closely related to having better listening skills throughout the system is that the mentally ill need a "witness" to their stories and suffering. By "witness" I mean the opportunity to tell our stories at length, both the good and the bad. This needs to be done in a setting without judgment where there is support, time and empathy. We need to be validated for both our pain and our triumphs without it being a complaint session. This too could be a low cost intervention. As Dr. Rachel Naomi Remen said, "What often makes the difference in treatment (of chronic or life-threatened illness) is not the right drug but the right story." (Remen, 2004)

Bits and pieces of our stories come out in support groups or even hospital therapy groups, but I am suggesting a different setting, professionally handled, so that it doesn't deteriorate into an "Ain't It Awful" symposium. Swiss psychoanalyst and author, Alice Miller, addressed this concept of witness in her discussion of how it saves abused children. People like Hitler, Stalin and Hussein lacked the empathetic witness to their childhood when they were suffering from severe abuse. Thus, it was totally suppressed, acted out later in rage upon the public. Dr. Edward Tick, who has spent more than 30 years working with veterans, is another who describes the value of "witness." He facilitates it in sweat lodges and on healing trips to Vietnam and other places. Soldiers loaded with PTSD are healed when they have the chance to air the stories about the horrors of war that usually lie buried.

For years I was loaded with the horror and trauma of my path. I was full of shame and pain. A brief relationship with a man who also suffered from manic depression for 26 years helped heal me. Even without discussing things in detail, I knew he understood; the fact that he did helped me accept the trauma without so much shame. His presence lessened the stigma, helped free me from the memories of madness.

One of the most disturbing things about mental illness is the fact that there are more ill people in prisons than in mental health institutions. This is because of the de-institutionalization movement years ago. 80 percent of state mental hospital residents were released. Vulnerable people were literally dumped on the streets where they reside today, or else many are in jails and prisons. (Earley, 2006) Today it is estimated that at least 26 percent of inmates in jails and prisons have a serious mental illness. "America's jails and prisons have once again become our mental hospitals." (Pavle June 2010 Public Citizen's Health Research Group Health Letter).

Now there is virtually nothing to deal with a prisoner's mental illness. Many are drugged into submission or otherwise live in abominable circumstances on cell blocks. Peter Earley has documented this tragedy in *Crazy: A Father's Search Through America's Mental Health Madness.* According to Earley, there is a web of bureaucracy, bad judgments and apathy that results in brutal conditions and little hope for recovery. "Instead of care, they get confinement. Instead of treatment, they get a trip through the 'revolving doors' between hospital and jail".

Beyond the tragedy of our criminal justice system's treatment of the mentally ill, there are two ways that mental illness could be treated radically differently. Both would undoubtedly reduce the costs of these illnesses substantially. They involve relying much less on hospitals by treating people in residential settings. The other idea is to establish comprehensive "wellness centers" where education about the new paradigm and treatment methods could take place. Some alternative methods would be available, chosen with supervision but mostly by the clients themselves. There is a body of wisdom that guides us. We move toward what we need when we are ready. The old saying is "when the student is ready the teacher appears." To be educated about certain approaches versus prescribed them, but advised about them and followed afterwards with support, could do wonders for the mentally ill. Such wellness centers are definitely applicable to other illnesses as well. But why should we segregate the mentally ill? The fact that 19 million suffer from depression qualifies as an epidemic, but we lack centers for such things while we are overloaded with cancer and heart centers. Depression costs at least 44 billion and manic depression 45 billion, yet there is supposedly no money in the system for widespread treatment.

Included in the offerings would be up-to-date nutrition education, not the pablum usually dispensed, plus naturopathic approaches, bodywork and energy healing. Hellinger Family Constellation work could be institutionalized.

Some medical centers are beginning to move in this direction to treat other illnesses. They offer acupuncture, massage, energy healing and counselors. Some elements of what could be an expanded wellness center exist outside the healthcare system at the Franciscan Spirituality Center in La Crosse. They offer Tai Chi, meditation, Reiki, Yoga, a depression group, lectures on mysticism, and retreats. The Center, however, is separated from their hospital wellness center and is a place where most mentally ill people would not feel comfortable. Nor are they specifically invited. The fact that there are reduced fees available is not well known.

Despite the fact that some approaches would cost money, the end result would undoubtedly be cost-effective. With a new belief system and the tools to significantly improve our wellness, there would be fewer hospitalizations or such lengthy ones, more economic productivity possible, less disrupted lives, less trauma and pain and fewer suicides. Wellness centers would be places where hope reigns supreme, along with education, support and mentoring that overloaded caseworkers now try to provide alone.

Other wellness methods could be offered at no or low cost, such as journaling, grief groups, etc. (See Chapter 7: Search for Healing.) The director of such a place would need to be both innovative and/or an educator, rotating the curriculum to different offerings throughout the year. Clients themselves might become teachers or facilitators with the right support. The whole community, not just the mentally ill, could go there and benefit. Integrated medicine would be the norm. Integrated programs are making inroads in such hallowed places as Duke University and Andrew Weil's University of Arizona program, but they are still implemented in too small a way, at a snail's pace, not yet available to the mentally ill.

The residential facility I envision could be a place where nature is close at hand and where patients can participate in the work of the facility. Several times I would have leaped at the chance to be part of something like this, including on an out-patient basis. I needed to restore the connections within myself; I could have done that easier, faster, by taking care of plants or gardening. I needed to touch things and become grounded. I needed community and support. I needed time to rest; I needed to feel valued, whether it was cooking or cleaning or gardening, especially when I couldn't work in the outside world.

Such gardening experiments have been successful with prisoners, giving them something to occupy their time as well as the chance to restore self-esteem. Hospitals are still needed for crisis stabilization, but the extended stays could be lessened; the residential facility concept where profound healing is possible could replace current mediocre attempts to place people in halfway houses. What is most lacking for the mentally ill is education, healing tools and support for *after* we leave a hospital. Few people would be able to do on their own what I did to get well; I had advantages and motivation that are rare.

The model for a residential facility should examine the work of John Weir Perry, a progressive psychiatrist who practiced and wrote in the 1950s and 60s. He established a house where those suffering from schizophrenia and manic depression were allowed to experience their episodes. The staff was trained just to "be with" the clients in listening and support. Nature was close at hand, even in the city; art expression was also available. What Perry found was that mythic experiences were often identifiable in this unusual setting; if the episode was allowed to run its course with such non-judgment and support, people often emerged healed. So far I have yet to find a psychiatrist who has even read Perry. Medications management seems their sole tool. This must be boring for doctors. It is very, very expensive, and it is troubling for many patients who suffer side effects. We deserve much more in the way of help to heal.

Another thing that could be done is to gather a number of the low or no cost methods from my list, incorporating them into a treatment program for the mentally ill, including prisoners. There are stories of convicts who have healed themselves with meditation, been helped with support groups, and pursued education of various kinds. Most of them have time on their hands. Imagine a group of prisoners trained to use EFT exercises. Perhaps such a view is naïve, but why not? A model program of recovery tools could be developed. Education alone might help some to dare to hope that they can escape their mental illness "sentences." Anything would be better than the current situation where they are sentenced not only to their crimes but often to serious madness exacerbated by their lack of treatment. Little is being done for them except knocking them out with medications.

Unfortunately, the larger medical model and mental health system is unlikely to shift soon to such enlightened treatment. The power of a *model*, however, should be pursued in places where there is some readiness. As Margaret Wheatley, author of *Leadership and the New Science* points out, a small system is the place to start. "Our activities in one part of the whole create non-local causes that emerge far from us. There is value in working in the system any place it manifests because unseen connections will create effects at a distance, in places we never thought. This model of change - of small starts, surprises, unseen connections, quantum leaps - matches our experience more closely

than our favored models of incremental change."
(Wheatley, 1994)

In a smaller way I put together my own hodge-
podge model of healing over nine years. I did it largely
on my own, without supervision or traditional support,
but I experienced many small surprises, unseen
connections and quantum leaps. Despite extraordinary
hospitalizations and hardship, I believe I was called to
travel a severe path in order to bring back these ideas
so that others might have an easier time. I was
unusually well equipped to do so because of the
advantages of my life, but the adversity was also
horrendous. Through it all, however, I managed to keep
hope alive even if only sporadically, and I am well today
in extraordinary ways. I believe thousands more can be
well too with similar help, self-responsibility, system
support and even one fourth the tools I used. Someday
I would like to help establish a healing center and
consult with those wanting to establish progressive
programs.

Alice A. Holstein

A Tough Grace

Tough Grace is a gift from God to the soul in need of growth.

Wayne Teasdale, *A Monk in the World,* p.166

Chapter 10: Gifts of Tough Grace

Some of the gifts of my illness are already evident in this book. They can also be called spiritual lessons, for they amount to a journey toward faith, a profound spiritual path. As Wayne Teasdale says, so often we do not know until later what the gifts have been. Only suffering and reflection make them clear.

One of the most helpful tools I found to help me *re-frame* my experiences was the tape on "Spiritual Madness" by Caroline Myss. It came into my hands at just the right time. I listened to that tape at least three times to be able to hand copy her words. Then I pored over the notes to be able to anchor them inside. Myss suggests that spirituality is usually portrayed as something sweet and easy, gained through piety and prayer. These cannot be discounted, but she points out that more often spirituality is full of hardship and pain. There we are tested and tried. There we are taught things such as humility, surrender, endurance and facing all our fears. Wayne Dyer is another who states unequivocally that changing our beliefs about life changes everything. It's how we hold something that counts, not the usual "Ain't It Awful" stance.

This stance is not likely to come easily or quickly. According to Fritz Kunkel, an important but little-known psychotherapist, there is a staging process similar to Joseph Campbell's hero's journey. First there is regression and reintegration. He believed it was the time when the rigid structure of the former life collapses. The second stage of the journey is turning toward the center, but we do so with a still small frame of reference. Here our fears are turned to anxiety. The third stage is "illumination." Intellectual insight is part of our new eyes, but is also an emotional experience, a change in our beliefs and choices that overthrows the whole system of our values, goals and means. It changes our whole viewpoint. We shift from being less conscious and egocentric to a well-centered life pivoting around the real Self. "The crisis, if it is complete, means conversion." (Kunkel/Sanford, 1984) Such a conversion happened to me, and with it a profound degree of wellness. Among my other spiritual gifts were the following:

An Expanded Purpose

My career up to the point of diagnosis in 1995 had always been value-based, in that I was motivated by helping people and facilitating systems change to create a more humane, participatory work environment. Now, however, I know that everything in my life has had meaning and purpose. The pursuit of psychological knowledge, whether about people or systems, has been related to the lessons of surviving mental illness. Indeed, the latter is the capstone that only now allows me to be an effective voice in the world. At age 65 I became employed once again as a peer support specialist with the Veteran's Administration. This means I deal with veterans on a "been there, done that" basis and I know it makes a difference.

I also know that I must tell my story and speak for the voiceless ones. It has been my privilege to do quite a bit of that the last few years so that I know that my treacherous path can bring hope and enlightenment to others. As I approach older age, I know that the rest of my life must be devoted to service and that I am ready to speak my truth in ways I never did before because I have been steeled to the task. My beliefs come from my heart and belly with no small amount of fire, brimstone and strength.

Developing Life Skills

I eat differently from what I did before. My body likes the effects, rebelling when I retreat to former habits. I do grief exercises when needed and gratitude recitations nightly. I use healers when I recognize a signal that there is more work to do. I am careful to get enough sleep and to not take on too much in my daily schedule. I insist on quiet time and live relatively simply. I am involved in my community and have good sources of support and stimulation.

Deepened Compassion and Empathy

Never again will I pass a bag lady, a homeless person, a drunk, a mentally ill or disabled person, an unkempt soul or anyone suffering with the judgment I once possessed. I was one of them, and walking in their shoes opened my heart spiritually. My compassion for the human race has been enlarged considerably.

Appreciation for Things Large and Small

Later in my journey I adopted the habit of counting daily blessings before sleep at night. Often the list does not get finished before sleep arrives. The gratitude ranges from thanks for a good tasting salad to a phone call from someone to appreciation for my home and clothes and my bed. Peace of mind is on the list too, and deep gratitude for a new life to live. In general,

I am thankful to be alive at all, much less to have such a promising future in my later middle age. Each day is precious in a way it never was before. And I try to extend this appreciation to others because of knowing what a kind word, a smile, a genuine thank you can mean. I know that I have a light to shine in this world and that I can use it in ways large and small.

Letting Go of Control

Because of my journey I am much more apt to consider things that happen or don't happen in life as nothing but signals to go a certain direction or turn to another path. I don't push the river, shrugging off things more easily. My energy leads me to things rather than what "should" be done.

One of the steps in any 12-Step program deals with letting go of control. Trusting the flow, I am more accepting of what *is* these days. I trust my intuition, my thoughts and answers at a deep level. Controlling things or people is not as important as paying attention and following the signals to respond. I merge this with my will, creating good days and a future.

Using Anger Constructively

In 1998 I got angry at the doctors for their limited treatment methods, their attitudes and their messages of hopelessness. I am still angry about much of our broken healthcare system, both in its belief system and its life-denying practices and structures. I do my best to remember that many in this system are merely unconscious, not necessarily bad people. Not attacking them is important. Nonetheless, there is a place for righteous anger.   My job is to speak my truth as effectively as possible.

But speak out I must.   There are many strong statements to make.   Challenging people can mean being a catalyst for discovering deeper truths. I am here to be a revolutionary, albeit a non-violent one.   Many spiritual leaders counsel forgiveness as a primary attitude, but somewhere between forgiveness and attack there is a place to say NO to abuse, ignorance and inhumanity. There is a place for upsetting people's comfort zone by putting such anger behind me, in the small of my back, so that it moves me out into the world where I write and speak without timidity. Indeed, I bear the burden of speaking my truth, knowing that it may be scorned or rejected.   Such truth is aimed at the complacent and the unjust. It may be accepted or not, but it is intended to be the tough love that helps people grow and change.

Knowing and Practicing Humility

A friend came to me recently to share his pain about feeling spiritually stuck. I was grateful that he honored me with his trust, and humbled that he would seek me out after I had invaded his space several times with phone calls that had been made from the depths of my madness. Another time there was a letter from a woman I met in a psych ward who said my compassion and hope had saved her life during some moments of extreme despair. Humbled by her admission, I was grateful there had been wisdom to share.

Humility is a difficult concept to describe; it is not self-effacing, but the dictionary does say that it means to be "modest." Such feelings exist alongside my claim to a "warrior's badge," to the quiet pride felt in surviving this journey and the terribly hard work to survive it with aplomb. But I am modest about that too, recognizing the grace received every step of the way.

Taking Care of Myself

I have much more patience than I ever had before. I had to learn time and again not to push myself too hard, to take care of all of my needs, meaning physical, mental, emotional and spiritual. I know how to say NO to things and people in ways I never did before. At one point in my recovery, I was so fragile that it became necessary to retreat until some strength could be restored. Slowly adding things to my schedule, I began to create a new life without some of the obligations that were weighing me down. In other words, I know my boundaries better than ever, and it is easier to ask for what I need or want.

Being Able to Love

Before I did the rigorous work of healing the wounds of my dysfunctional past, as well as the wounds of the culture, I did not know how to love very well. There were too many holes in my soul. My buttons were pushed too easily. Over the years I had a number of failed relationships with men. They were all part of my learning, but there has been time for reflection about the lessons. Especially when I healed my mother connection in early 2003 through a Hellinger Family Constellation workshop, I knew that my capacity to love had been restored.

A Tough Grace

Facing and Accepting Death

I must have faced death of various kinds hundreds of times along the path. The suffering was almost unendurable for seven years; the mental, physical, emotional and spiritual exhaustion continued periodically for twelve years; the physical danger was real many times; the stress was chronic. In addition, I had a profound near-death experience that feels comparable to that borne by Shamans. In a very real sense, I, like them, healed myself from serious illness with a lot of help from others. Thus, I am no longer afraid of my own actual death. If it should come tomorrow, I can rest easy that I survived this illness although I would be terribly sad to miss the rest.

Finding Wisdom and Creativity

Finding William Styron's thoughts that illness was the opening to wisdom seemed like a true but odd thought. It was odd then because I was still brainwashed with that "Ain't It Awful" attitude from friends, the professionals and myself. The fruits of the journey had not been fully claimed.

Deepened wisdom first emerged in 2002 when I began to reclaim my life in earnest by reading voraciously and distilling experiences. It grew stronger as time went on, despite more episodes. Wisdom is the power to digest experiences quickly and deeply. It is the gift of seeing the essence of people and situations beneath the surface and to make superior decisions for oneself. It is the focus to sort out priorities easily based upon knowledge, experience and understanding.

Wisdom is frequently found in older people; they have perspective; they have reflected about their lives and learned many lessons, yet there are many unwise elders whose lives became frozen at an earlier age. My wisdom seemed to progress apace with my healing; soon it became noticeable to others too. A new level of depth and meaning came through. One of the most special gifts is having had the time to distill things because of an interrupted life, but I was also forced to the task in order to make sense out of it all. The wisdom feels like an enhanced ability to penetrate easily to the heart of things. Manic depression forced me to an expanded consciousness that transforms everything.

Increased creativity is another blessing. Before I did my mid-life inner work, I was a bright person but a plodder. I worked hard for every accomplishment. My creativity, however, began to shine through in my mid-40s as I wrote a book and became a better organization consultant. Now, after surviving mental illness, my creativity is strong. This book was written in draft form in several weeks. The words spilled onto the pages. I have written other things in stream of consciousness that needed very little editing. Otherwise I am able to put together dissimilar thoughts in dissimilar ways, one of the definitions of creativity. I feel able to live creatively in simple but meaningful ways. My intuition is very strong and very useful. I am following my bliss, as Joseph Campbell would say.

Tapping Core Self-knowledge

Finally, everything about this journey has contributed to a core of self-knowledge that feels very deep and rooted. As my friend, Maria, says, you find out who you are when your back is against the wall. I know my capacity for suffering. I know what I endured and that I am both fragile and very, very strong. I know the people and events that "saved" me countless times. I know how listening heals. I know what I claim as my own dogged work. I know how much has been grace. I know the sources and depth of my faith. I see that this illness has been a profound journey to the soul, a blessed path.

Alice A. Holstein

So many of us do not know our own story. A story about who we are, not what we have done. About what we faced to build what we have built, what we have drawn upon and risked to do it, what we have thought, felt and feared and discovered through the events of our lives. The real story that belongs to us alone.

Rachel Naomi Remen
Kitchen Table Wisdom p. xxvii

Chapter 11: Whole in One

I don't know exactly when or how I slipped into a new place in my body during the summer of 2005. Of course it had been building for years. The shift emerged subtly, making me feel as though I was burrowing into a new center of safety as I sat on my sofa one morning. While working with some study notes, something in the words gently tipped the balance. Suddenly I "got," in a comprehensive way, what manic depression had been about and why it had been my destiny to bear its pain.

During the next week the avalanche of insight continued. Instinctively I turned to several favorite books. Jungian Marion Woodman's thoughts about befriending the dark Goddess in *Dancing in the Flames* took on new meaning. She suggested that finding a new, more conscious feminine is often accompanied by illness. Only suffering makes us whole, she proclaimed, and most of us are dragged toward wholeness. Aha! I thought, finally someone with her depth sees the positive side of illness rather than judging symptoms as "bad" or "terrible," easily fixed with pills. I certainly understood what being dragged toward wholeness meant, and I wished, wistfully, that others did too. For years I had suffered with mental illness with an almost

100% negative label about it in my mind. With Woodman's insights, I realized that I was tapping into a crucial reclaiming of the feminine that represents a consciousness level heretofore unknown. This insight is especially important because we are a civilization cut off at the neck, full of intellectual knowledge but disconnected from both ourselves and nature. I did not understand this disembodiment factor until the illness led me to Woodman and Morris Berman who wrote *Coming To Our Senses.* Without better physical grounding we remain a schizoid society. Woodman suggests that the feminine energy is identified with soul, the embodied part of the eternal, while masculine is identified with the spirit, the disembodied aspect of each person. Healing the rift between mind and body is what can heal the ailing unconscious of the patriarchy. The fact that it remains unconscious creates the personal, political and social ills around us.

Jungian Robert Johnson, in *Femininity Lost and Regained* and historian Richard Tarnas' *The Passion of the Western Mind* write of this evolution too, pointing out that the marriage of the feminine and masculine within creates a new level of wholeness. Why is this concept so missing from popular culture when the self-destruction of a pervasive masculine remains so strong? I also read Barbara Walker's book, *Crone,* on elder wise women, wondering why my first reading years ago had left me so cold. Now I claimed her truth, that so many of our leaders, often male, otherwise qualified by background and experience, lack the psychological maturity to make decisions on behalf of the species.

The source of my study notes that day was Willis Harman, esteemed scientist, futurist and co-founder of the World Business Academy. This wise, understated man talked about the wholeness that was emerging in society via a shift from *external* authority to *inner* authority. He suggested that this was the underlying change that was so important beneath the symptoms of breakdown during tumultuous transition times. Harman reinforced my belief that doing our inner work was so essential, although too few know of it or find the help to navigate its sometimes rough waters. In the meantime, we remain immature, egocentric, outer-directed and unfulfilled people. Our world view remains mired in the old values and habits that are destroying the world. The mainstream lacks transformation, whether personal, organizational or societal.

All these sources and more reinforced the conclusion that my tortuous bout with manic depression had been a whole body, whole person illness, not the limited brain disease that doctors treat almost solely with drugs. Now I understood that enduring this bone-crushing path did indeed have an underlying wholeness. It took me to the collective unconscious to heal myself and to retrieve deeply repressed qualities necessary for a new consciousness level. There were personal issues to heal, of course, but something bigger was occurring. I had lived out the mind-body split of civilization in the extreme. I had healed not only the inner wounds but was making a contribution to the collective in general.

The prize upon return is the wisdom and personal power of a missing part of the female trinity, the elder wise woman energy that was almost totally obliterated during the 12th to the 18th centuries when some nine million women were killed. This unbalanced feminine-masculine, fully-embodied energy, is still virtually absent today. Some women, however, and a few men are recovering it, finding in the process new strength to stand strong against the patriarchy with its skewed version of reality and history. My word for this new era in history is the "Humanarchy," which cannot unfold without this retrieval of the soul to balance masculine spirit. The new consciousness cannot exist without the feminine LOVE principle to transform greed and unjust power. As Woodman points out, it is not masculinity that is at fault. That is the creative energy of the universe. The patriarchy, however, has become a power complex. Not only are the rich and powerful under this spell; both women and men seduced by materialism are as well. The patriarchy, beginning some 4,500 years ago, has been an essential stage in history, but its time is finished. The trouble is that many do not realize it yet. They are hanging on for dear life to the ego defenses that characterize a still dominant masculine consciousness. As I sat on the couch, finding a new center in myself, I wanted to shout to the world that it is time to grow up, to get over it before we destroy ourselves.

As the week wore on, I felt my spine straighten and rearrange itself into a new sense of inner strength. A profound reintegration, a harvesting of self and wisdom was unraveling. Quiet joy came over me. Since 1995 I'd been on an unbelievably rocky, wild ride through a living Hell, including constant trauma, physical endangerment, frequent despair and confrontations with death. Now I understood why the dismemberment had been so thorough. These were the tests and trials of a hero's journey, a prelude to bringing back something new to civilization. I had forged a holistic view of manic depression and how treatment could be changed to promote deep healing. I had realized that mental illness can be a profound spiritual path. The illness had burned me clean. I prayed for the physical strength to go forward, for I was still recovering from the black abyss and the tough grace that had guided me "home" to this new place in my soul.

My reverie reminded me of a mystical experience I'd had in 1980, when I heard the words, "It's time for love" floating mysteriously from the walls one evening. This was a mystical event rather than a hallucination. I didn't understand it then, and I forgot about it for 22 years until the words came back several years ago. Now the words meant a genuinely new era in history. They represented transforming breakdown to breakthrough. They promise wholeness for people everywhere. If enough of us do this work, we can catalyze the course correction of a planet fallen into its own abyss, facing extinction. The work is more than a "new age" mind shift. Underlying the shift in world view is an embodiment process that makes enlightened people a tuning fork for others. Such presence and balance is desperately needed today.

There is much madness in the world. It is irrational, deadly and destructive. The feminine LOVE principle must stand firm and hold. The patriarchy, as it has played itself out in both women and men, must be held accountable. We are frighteningly off course. The power complex of a masculine run amok has been too long in charge. Both woman and men have been wounded through the centuries. In order to become intellectually developed as a species, the feminine had to be negated. Patriarchy is not a bad word. The work of recovery, however, pushing us toward wholeness and an entirely new era, is now critical. Whether or not we avert disaster depends upon how many wake up from materialism, addictions, fear, complacency. The consciousness of each person matters desperately. Our maturation as a society has been in motion for a long time, but intensely so for at least 40 years. Only the generation of the 1960s and beyond has had the opportunity en masse to heal our evolutionary incompleteness. Often pain and illness take us to the psychological maturity that is our birthright. The prize can be human wholeness, planetary healing and a second Renaissance. My path has been a bone-crushing one, but I *choose* to call it tough grace and that has made all the difference.

Alice A. Holstein

Bibliography

Abdu'l-Baha. From a letter written on behalf of Shoghi Effendi, *Unfolding Destiny*. (1981) From the Internet site of Brian Kurzuis, www.hiddengifts.com , who has compiled quotes on the nature and purpose of tests and suffering, 2007.

Berman, Morris. *Coming to Our Senses.* New York: Bantam, 1989.

Campbell, Joseph with Moyers, Bill. *The Power of Myth.* New York: Doubleday, 1988. p.124

Campbell, Joseph, *Mythos Part II.* "The Spirit Land," video series. Unipax Entertainment & William Free Productions: The Joseph Campbell Foundation, 1986.

Chittester, Joan. *Scarred By Struggle.* Grand Rapids, MI: Wm.B. Eerdmans Publishing Co., 2005.

Chopra, Deepak. *Grow Younger, Live Longer,* New York. Harmony Books, 2001.

Cole, Ellen and Ochshorn, Judith. *Women's Spiritual Journey, Women's Lives.* Taylor and Francis, Inc., 1995

Cousineau, Editor. *Joseph Campbell: The Hero's Journey.* Novato, CA: New World Library, 1990. p. 137

Dyer, Wayne. *The Power of Intention.* PBS Presentation, 8/18/04.

Frattaroli, Elio. *Healing the Soul In the Age of the Brain.* New York: Viking, 2001.

Glassey, Donald J. "Bodywork and Neuropeptides - The Molecules of Healing." Internet article, 2010.

Grof, S. & Grof, C. *Beyond the Brain.* London: Thames and Hudson, 1980. p 322

Hammerschlag, Carl A. and Silverman, Howard D. *Healing Ceremonies.* New York: Perigree-Berkley Publishing Group, 1997.

Hammerschlag, Carl A. *The Theft of the Spirit.* *New York: Simon & Schuster, 1993.*

Hanh, Thich Nhat. Creating True Peace. New York: Free Press, 2003.

Hellinger Family Constellation work with Peter deVries in La Crosse, WI (2003) and Viroqua, WI (2005). www.Constellationworks.com. See also Hellinger Constellation work as a general search engine entry.

Herman, Judith Lewis, *Trauma and Recovery.* Basic Books, Harper Collins, 1992.

International Children's Bible. Dallas: Word Publishing, 1988.

Johnson, Robert. *Femininity Lost and Regained.* New York: Harper & Row, 1990.

_____. Lecture to Jung Society, Tucson, AZ 1988.

Kunkel, Fritz. *Selected Writings With An Introduction and Commentary by John A. Sanford.* New York: Paulist Press, 1984. pp.266-5

Levine, Peter (with Ana Frederick). *Waking the Tiger.* Berkeley, CA: North Atlantic Books, 1997.

Mack, Alice H. *Beyond Turmoil.* Tucson, AZ: Connexions Unlimited, 1992.

Maslow, Abraham H. *Motivation and Personality, 2nd Edition.* New York: Harper & Row, 1954,1970.

Miller, Alice. *Banished Knowledge.* New York: Doubleday, 1990.

_____. *The Body Never Lies.* New York: W.W. Norton & Co., 2005

_____. www.alice-miller.com (book list plus articles)

Mines, Stephanie. *We Are All In Shock.* Franklin Lakes, N.J.: New Page Books, 2003.

Myss, Caroline. *Why People Don't Heal and How They Can.* Video Recording, Inner Dimension, 1997.

_____. *Spiritual Madness.* Tape Recording. Boulder, CO: Sounds True, 1999.

MacLaine, Shirley. *The Camino.* New York: Pocket Books, 2000.

Nasar, Sylvia. *A Beautiful Mind.* New York: Touchstone, 1998.

Peat, F. David. *Infinite Potential: The Life and Times of David Bohn:* Reading, MA: Addison Wesley, 1997. p.318

Perry John Weir. *The Far Side of Madness.* Dallas, TX: Spring Publications, 1973.

_____ *Roots of Renewal in Myth and Madness.* San Francisco: Jossey-Bass Publishers, 1976.

_____ *The Self In Psychotic Process.* Dallas, TX: Spring Publications, 1973

Pert, Candace B. *Molecules of Emotion.* New York: Touchstone, 1997.

Reiss, Marguerite. *Holy Nudges.* Denver, CO: Logos Int'l, 1976.

Remen, Rachel Naomi. *Kitchen Table Wisdom.* New York: Riverhead Books, 1996.

Remen, Rachel Naomi, Interview on ABC local affiliate (La Crosse, WI) Channel 9, December 20, 2004

Ruppert Franz. *Systemic Solutions,* Psychosis and Schizophrenia: Disturbed Bonding in the Family System." Englewood Road, London SW12PPB, England. Issue 3, 2002. pp.17-19.

Sanford, John A. *The Kingdom Within.* San Francisco: Harper & Row, 1987.

_____. *Healing Body and Soul.* Louisville, KY: Westminster/John Knox Press, 1992.

_____. *The Man Who Wrestled With God.* New York: Paulist Press, 1974, 1981.

Styron, William. *Darkness Visible.* New York: Random House, 1990.

Tarnas, Richard. *The Passion of the Western Mind.* New York: Ballantine Books, 1991.

Teasdale, Wayne. *A Monk in the World.* Novato, CA: New World Library, 2002. p.167.

Tick, Ed. *War and the Soul.* Wheaton, IL. Quest Books, 2005

Underhill, Evelyn. *The Essentials of Mysticism and Other Essays.* New York: E.P. Dutton and Co., 1920.

Walker, Barbara G. *The Crone.* New York: Harper Collins, 1985.

Wheatley, Margaret. *Leadership and the New Science.* San Francisco: Berrett-Koehler, 1994. p. 42-3.

Woodman, Marion. *Bone: Dying Into Life.* Viking Compass, 2000.

_____. *Dancing In the Flames.* Boston: Shambala. 1996.

_____. *Sitting By The Well.* Boulder, CO: Sounds True, 1991-96, 6 tapes

Young, Robert O. and Young, Shelley Redford. *The PH Miracle.* New York: Warner Books, 2002.

CPSIA information can be obtained at www.ICGtesting.com
Printed in the USA
LVOW071053100212

268091LV00001B/2/P